D0913738

CONQUERING PORNOGRAPHY
OVERCOMING THE ADDICTION

DR. DENNIS FREDERICK

Written with Jo Marie Dooley

CONQUERING PORNOGRAPHY
OVERCOMING THE ADDICTION

A Practical, Faith-Based Journey
by Dennis Frederick, M.Div., Ph.D.

Pleasant Word
A Division of WINEPRESS PUBLISHING

Pleasant Word (a division of WinePress Publishing, PO Box 428, Enumclaw, WA 98022) functions only as book publisher. As such, the ultimate design, content, editorial accuracy, and views expressed or implied in this work are those of the author.

NOTE: This book is based on years of therapeutic practice. No actual names or personal stories are used and any similarities to real people or events are coincidental.

Unless otherwise noted, all Scriptures are taken from the Holy Bible, New International Version, Copyright © 1973, 1978, 1984 by the International Bible Society. Used by permission of Zondervan Publishing House. The "NIV" and "New International Version" trademarks are registered in the United States Patent and Trademark Office by International Bible Society.

ISBN 13: 978-1-4141-0617-5
ISBN 10: 1-4141-0617-3
Library of Congress Catalog Card Number: 2005910183

DEDICATION

This book is dedicated to all the men and women who have shared their struggle with pornography and helped me learn how they have overcome. May God continue to lead them along paths of righteousness and bless their lives abundantly.

And to my dear wife, Dr. Glenna Frederick, for her patience, kindness, and loving support in not only this project but also our life's journey together.

TABLE OF CONTENTS

FOREWORD

I have known Dr. Dennis Frederick and his family for many years and have seen his faithful commitment to serve the Lord through his psychotherapeutic practice, his pastoral work, and his daily Christian walk. When Dr. Frederick initially considered writing this book, he came to me as his pastor and friend to discuss the growing need he saw among men who were succumbing to the temptation of pornography. We talked about what I had encountered among the people, churches, and pastors I know, and we agreed that an addiction to pornography had caused the destruction of many marriages and careers. I encouraged him to pursue his vision for this book and believe it is a project ordained and blessed by God.

Conquering Pornography: Overcoming the Addiction is a well-written and valuable tool that individuals and groups will use to address pornography's stronghold on men. These are not horrible men; they represent all the various cultures and elements of our American society. When Jesus conducted his earthly ministry, he did not spend the majority of his time associating with the wealthy, the healthy, and the spiritually well-adjusted. Instead he sought the company of the poor, the sick, and those who, due to their sins, were marginalized from families, society, and their relationship with God.

Therefore, it doesn't matter if you are deeply involved in using pornography, because Christ sacrificed his life that you might live more abundantly and in freedom from this addiction. We know that everyone is a sinner; but we also know that Christ is the Redeemer. If you will follow the steps outlined in this book, your life, your marriage, and your future can be redeemed.

I pray that you will be transformed as you read the words in this book. May God bless you as you work to rebuild that which pornography has taken from you.

Ben Cross, D.Min.
Senior Pastor
Grace Community Church

ACKNOWLEDGMENTS

To accomplish a project like the creation of this book takes the hands, hearts, minds, and, most important, the prayers of many, many people. While the book originated in my head—with a strong leading of the Holy Spirit that it needed to be written—the work to bring the idea to fruition involved the dedicated labor of the following people:

- Dr. Glenna Frederick, my wonderful wife, Director of Curriculum and Staff Development at Cascade Christian Schools, who read every word and offered unique and insightful input into the book.
- Jo Marie Dooley, editor, who shared my vision for this book and provided her invaluable skills by translating my ideas and words into cohesive sentences. I appreciate the long hours she dedicated to this project and pray that she will be blessed by the lives that will be touched through her efforts.

- Lee Webb, Tern Christian Counseling office manager, for her efforts to keep our practice in order while I worked on the book.
- Gregory Gates, associate therapist, for his excellent research skills that brought substance to my ideas.
- George Hetherington, Tern associate, for his professional support and spiritual counsel as well as his belief in the need for this project.
- Robin Webb, associate therapist, for her discernment regarding spiritual warfare and her conviction as a prayer warrior.
- My sons Eric and Ryan (and his lovely wife, Selena) and my parents Gorden and JoAnn for their constant encouragement and help in keeping me on track.
- Reverend Dr. Ben Cross, senior pastor of Grace Community Church in Auburn, Washington, and board member of Tern, who offered encouragement and affirmed what the Holy Spirit was leading me to do and wrote the foreword for this book.
- Clarice Knoll, Mr. and Mrs. Shawn Manley, Chuck Maples, Doug Pendergraft and Deanna Pendergraft, Greg and Raelene Sutherland, Russ Wilson, and The Duus Family—by sharing their financial resources, I was able to focus on writing this book.

INTRODUCTION

When it comes to counseling, I don't deal with drug addicts or street people or criminals. Tern Christian Counseling's clients are families and individuals who come with a variety of issues and problems. I began this practice in 1987, and over the years—in response to the growing need—my specialty has become sexual issues in men. This has evolved into addressing the problem of pornography due to its rampant growth. These Christian men whom I counsel—church leaders, pastors, husbands, and fathers—are from "normal" American homes. And they all have a terrible, life-threatening secret: an addiction to pornography.

Each year statistics reveal that in the United States alone, people spend $20 billion on adult videos and another $12 billion on print materials and phone sex. It is estimated that more than 4 million Web sites exist worldwide, catering to some 72 million people who want to view pornographic images at their home or office computer. Twenty percent of American men admit to accessing pornography while at work. Pornography is now a major problem in nearly 50 percent of all U.S. homes. And when asked, more than 50 percent of Christian men have recently visited a pornographic site.[*]

This provocative book is intended for a very specific audience. It is for men who seriously want to overcome their addiction to pornography. It applies to all types of sexual preferences and levels of addiction. Each person thinks he is unique and, therefore, alone. The message is this: You are not alone, but you feel isolated. This is part of the lie that is the addiction to pornography.

I have written these chapters based on what I have learned through thirty-plus years of clinical experience working specifically with men having sexual problems. The book is intended to be a practical approach. It is not a theoretical study. This is an upfront look addressing the serious issue of pornography in our homes. It seeks to provide some insightful methods to heal from the corruption pornography has caused in the hearts and lives of millions of men and their relationships.

Conquering Pornography: Overcoming the Addiction may be used as a self-study, but as with all addictions, there needs to be accountability. I recommend a group setting with two or more men. Content in the book is not meant for children of any age, unless they are addicted to pornography and have an understanding and healthy Christian male role model to help them work though this difficult and personal process. Women may want to read this book for information to support their husband or loved ones.

The foundational principles in this book come from a strong ecumenical Christian perspective. It does not judge the individual, but rather it looks at the sin as a sin, not an "issue." God is the only true means to find victory over this deep-rooted, personal war that rages inside each man who has felt its stronghold and tried to free himself on his own.

In addition to content addressing the many dimensions of addiction, I have included Scripture references for those who want to learn how much God wants you to be a whole and victorious person. The intent is to help you become aware of the sinful nature of the addiction, lead you to a spirit of repentance, encourage you in recovery, and enhance your relationship with God, with your spouse, and with your children.

If you are addicted to pornography, the battle to overcome will be long and difficult. It requires a serious commitment along with the motivation and fortitude to stick with the plan. Reading this book on a casual basis will only add information to your mind. However, applying the ideas and practical steps, as the Lord leads you, will change you into a much more complete and free individual. This choice is fully up to you. You cannot change because you were caught practicing your addiction and now someone else is making you seek help to overcome it. That motive will fade fast. It's often too late for men who come into therapy as the last resort because their wives threatened them with divorce papers. You must start the work before that point.

For those men who are willing to take the challenge and transform their hearts and minds, I want to say to you: Be encouraged. There is hope and healing. I have seen many men change and resume a normal, healthy lifestyle. God wants you to live a life of freedom and peace.

May this book start you on a whole new journey!

1. Scripture Reading: Philippians 3:20-21

*"Internet Pornography Statistics"; ©TopTenReviews; http://internet-filter-review.toptenreviews.com/internet-pornography-statistics.html; 08/15/2006.

INVENTORY:
Is This Book for Me?

If you are struggling with determining if you have an addiction to pornography, take a few minutes to complete the following self-assessment. Your responses will provide valuable insight into your habits and help identify the direction you want to take with your life.

Self-Assessment: Are You Addicted to Pornography?

		Disagree	Somewhat Agree	Agree
1.	I hide an adult movie or Web site from my wife or other family members and friends.			
2.	Pornography is like a comfortable, nonjudgmental friend when I feel lonely, frustrated, or stressed.			
3.	I masturbate when I watch pornography.			
4.	I look for opportunities to engage in pornography and look forward to engaging in it.			
5.	I have a predictable, confidential source for obtaining pornography.			

6.	I no longer feel like engaging in pornography is that big a deal.			
7.	What used to turn me on when I first started to watch pornography isn't enough to turn me on now.			
8.	I have particular preferences for what arouses me sexually (e.g., a particular ethnicity or body part, etc.).			
9.	I feel uncertain about my sexual performance, so engaging in pornography helps me achieve more confidence.			
10.	Although I have tried, I can't stop using pornography by sheer willpower.			
11.	I spend more time over the course of a week engaged in pornography than with my wife and children.			
12.	I have missed work or spent work time engaged in pornography.			
	TOTALS			

Even if you checked just one "Somewhat Agree" or "Agree," I encourage you to read this book.

CHAPTER 1

HOW YOU GOT HOOKED

The tall, distinguished-looking man in his late forties parks his car and casually walks toward the medical building full of dental offices. Jacob thanks God that he drives a plain Chevy instead of a flashy car so it won't be recognized. He brushes at the wrinkles in his expensive slacks and wishes the drive over the mountains didn't take two hours every week.

It's a nice day, but he has on a raincoat and fedora pulled down on his brow. As Jacob nears the door, he quickly scans the parking lot to ensure no one is watching. He enters the foyer and looks around for any familiar faces. Feeling confident that no one has seen him, he takes the back stairs two at a time and slips into my office, a bit breathless after three flights of stairs, and carefully closes the door behind him.

Without any preliminary greetings, we immediately proceed to my office. Jacob takes off his coat and hat, then sits in his usual chair to begin our regular therapy session. My patient is a well-known pastor and television personality, and he has been addicted to pornography for a decade. If his real name were known, his life would be ruined and the entire faith community rocked.

THE HISTORY OF PORNOGRAPHY

The history of pornography is as old as humankind. It has been found in the ruins of Pompeii where there are graphic statues and mosaic pictures. It has been found in ancient Egypt and China. It has been with man since the fall of Adam and Eve. There has been a history of pornography throughout all the great empires and in all countries worldwide.

If you were to look at recent history of the twentieth century, you would find that during the 1920s, 1930s, and 1940s, men had to go to a very specific bookstore in a major city or go to a theater that reeked of disinfectant to find the pornography they sought. A man had to sneak away from society to indulge his addiction…and prayed he would not get caught. Over the years, more discreet materials became available in the form of soft pornography. Magazines and pictures came through the mail, and over the years, the images became more graphic and more specialized in order to meet the requests of those with fetishes. In the later decades of the 20th century came easy access to videos that men could rent or own for a low price. A man could have anything he wanted in his own home and watch at his leisure.

Then came the Internet and the availability and volume of pornography exploded. A multi-billion-dollar industry was born, which has been supported by people doing whatever they wanted with no consequences. Men could keep their addiction private—no one needed to know. It was now free and so easily accessible. There was no limit to how many sites a user wanted to visit or the amount of time he spent on line. A man could go to international sites where U.S. laws could not dictate content. Whatever his wishes or desires, they could be fulfilled. All of this caused a rampant growth in the production and use of pornography.

Pornographic materials are now at an all-time high. Discussion about censorship is viewed as being in conflict with the U.S. Constitution. Filters and other accountability devices may be in place, but it's amazing how many "innocent" keywords trigger availability to a Web site filled with pornographic images. Someone even programmed the link whitehouse.com to take students to a pornography Web site. The people behind pornography are more clever than ever. They want to get you hooked because they make great profits off of you!

Points to Consider

1. Have you been drawn into using pornography?
2. What method do you use to access pornography?
3. What filters or what accountability methods are you willing to put in place to prevent growth of your addiction?

2. Scripture Reading: Judges 16:1

Soft Versus Hard Pornography

I n the industry, the difference is that soft pornography does not have the individuals engaging in full penetration sex acts. Hard pornography displays arousal and full penetration.

The bottom line: Pornography is pornography. The point is people often say that it's only soft pornography (for example, the magazines you can buy at the corner convenience store); it's not the triple-X material. Well, they are only one step away from each other. It's the effect on the heart and mind that is most important. So whether it's classified as "hard" or "soft" doesn't matter. What's critical is the level of attraction it has to you...the degree of hold it has on your life. Whatever you are using to become aroused is pornography. The labels are merely semantics.

Both soft and hard pornography are harmful. Both lead to the same dead end. They lead to the same hurts and destruction of the relationship. Don't use the rationale or the history of how you got hooked. Don't justify that because you use only soft pornography that your habit isn't *so* bad. It's all the same when it comes to addiction. Don't minimize or trivialize the effects that either soft or hard pornography has on your life.

Points to Consider

1. What pornography did you use in the beginning?
2. Have you progressed from the soft to the hard? Are you thinking of progressing to the hard or even more outrageous forms of pornography?

3. Are you being honest about the level of pornography you
    are currently using?

3. Scripture Reading: Proverbs: 27:20

What Is Appealing?

E very man has a preference when it comes to his attraction to women. Some men like legs, faces, breasts, or any other body parts. They prefer a certain color of hair or a particular ethnicity. That's why God made women in so many different shapes, sizes, and colors. It's natural for men to be attracted to specific types of women or certain physical attributes.

For some men, their attractions also feed their addiction. The man involved in pornography will spend an inordinate amount of time seeking images of women with a certain hair color or shape or age. They spend countless hours hunting for Web sites that feature a particular body part or pose.

Once you know what is appealing, you can zero in on how to modify your behavior and stop your addiction. For example, address the fact that you are drawn to the swimsuit or t-shirt editions of magazines. Know that these are things that trigger your addiction and make you want to look at materials or go to a particular Web site.

Oftentimes, what you find appealing has been taught to you. For example, a woman wearing stiletto heels may arouse you. As your addiction to pornography develops, you may form a connection between the stilettos and pornographic images. Then when you encounter a normal woman wearing high heels (even in a business setting), you get a sexual charge. Or perhaps you have associated women in certain types of uniforms with your sexual practices. Therefore, you become excited just by a simple encounter with a female nurse or police officer. The people in the pornography industry are extremely clever, and they have specific plans to lure you into multiple addictions. You become addicted to not only the sexual act or body part featured in the video, but also to what she is wearing, the music, the situation, or the lighting.

Points to Consider

1. Write down the specifics of what you are constantly looking for in pornographic materials.
2. What particular parts of a woman's body are you seeking graphic images of?
3. What other things have you now developed an attraction to because of your use of pornography?

4. Scripture Reading: Song of Songs: 4:1-5

How You Got Started

I t all started with one experience. Someone showed you a picture or you found a video. One young boy shared in a counseling session that he got started with pornography when he found materials in his next-door neighbor's recycling bin. He was on his way to school and spotted the magazine next to the tin cans and cardboard in the blue plastic box at the curb. He stuck the magazine in his backpack, and he had a steady supply of pornography every trash day.

One man in his thirties got started when he followed the link of a pop-up on his computer screen. He was checking his email, and the advertisement opened. He hit the "go" button, and there was the pornography. Someone else got started when a cousin showed him a video or a kid at camp sneaked some graphic pictures in his suitcase. Whatever the case, you saw it, you liked it, and your addiction was launched.

How does any addiction begin? Smoking—one cigarette at a time. Drinking—one beer at a time. Gambling—one bet at a time. It all seems innocent enough. You want to see what it feels like to smoke a cigarette. You want to taste beer or whiskey. You play poker, bet on a game, or play craps. At first the cost is small, but then the financial, physical, and emotional costs escalate. The pattern of addiction to pornography is the same. You tried it, you liked it, and you made it a part of your daily life.

But now you are in a place where you cannot stop on your own. You are in a place where you feel that you need help. The very fact that you are willing to read this book demonstrates that you are ready to step out and do something about your addiction to pornography.

An addiction to pornography can be stopped—but it's not as easy as how you got started. The tangled web has already encircled your heart, your soul, and your identity. The work will be difficult, but overcoming is possible and you can be free of this plague.

Points to Consider

1. Can you describe how you got started?
2. Who are the people who exposed you to pornography?
3. How far are you into the addiction?

5. *Scripture Reading: 1 John 2:16*

THE FOUR STAGES OF ADDICTION

The first stage of addiction is curiosity. A man may start by saying: "I was interested. I wanted to see what my friends were talking about, and I wanted to be able to relate with them." This may occur either as a child or an adult, but it is the male drive that says: "I want to see the forbidden fruit. Even though I know it's wrong, I want to just look. Just one look. I'll still be OK." Let me say that every man I have met is at some level curious about sex. It's healthy and natural. When it's channeled in the proper way, it leads to healthy sex education and appropriate actions. But it's at the "choice" phase when a male has to decide: "No, I don't want to go down that road. I want to choose the healthier road."

Nearly every guy I know reaches a crucial moment when he makes the decision which road he will choose. Here is a true illustration: Before there were personal computers and DVD rental stores, pornography was available in print, peep shows, or "blue" movies. One night a group of six college students got their hands on a couple of reels and scheduled a secret movie night. They hung a sheet on the wall in the lounge and cranked up the movie projector. At first their eyes were fixed on the images doing things they had never seen before. After a while it was time to switch reels. The lights came up, and four men left. They had seen enough. Their curiosity was satisfied. They made a choice not only to leave, but also for what they wanted to put into their minds and hearts. The rest stayed and wanted to do it on a regular basis. For them, the process to the next stage had begun. A year later some of the students who made pornography a regular part of their schedule went to a neighboring state where prostitution was legal. They acted out on their fantasies. Now thirty years later, it would be interesting to learn how that impacted their lives.

That leads to the next stage: dependency—dependency on the stimulation and dependency on a fantasy, which often relates to masturbation. There is dependency on the neuro-transmitters and endorphins that are produced when a person engages in sexual activity. The craving is fully present now, and he wants more of what he has become dependent upon. He also rationalizes and says to himself that what he is doing is not that big a deal and he can walk away from the pornography at any time. If this is the stage you are at and you don't feel you have become dependent, I challenge you to answer these questions: Why are you doing it every chance you get? Why do you look forward to the times when you can be alone and sit at the computer or go out of town so that you can watch movies in your hotel room? Dependency is the stage in which you communicate to yourself: "I am doing this because I want to on a regular basis."

Dependency then yields to addiction. Now the addiction controls you—your good sense and moral character are no longer in the driver's seat. Now you can't stop, and the desire for pornography has become destructive. You may be losing time at work. You may be losing time with your family. You are squeezing out other things that you used to love to do so that you can be involved in your addiction to pornography. You realize: "I can't stop. I have to do it all the time."

The fourth stage that comes out of addiction is acting out. Now the man wants to see his fantasies in real time. He will most likely demand more of his partner: "I want her to do the things I see on the computer. They may be disgusting to her, but I will coerce her into doing what I want through force or bribery or some form of emotional blackmail. But for me to be truly happy, I need her to perform what I saw. That's my goal. I want a three-way even though I know it's immoral and debauchery. Or maybe I need to hire a prostitute who could satisfy my needs and would be willing to act and moan and groan, doing the things I want done and telling me things I want to hear—even if she is faking it. Or perhaps you are now thinking that children would be appropriate sexual partners. They don't have such high expectations as adults. I could teach them. It would be a win-win for everyone. You now find yourself engaged in activities that are totally perverse and would disgust the majority of people. Furthermore, they may be illegal. All of this is part of acting out, and it all demonstrates the depths to which your addiction has taken you.

Statistics indicate that male criminals who initially said they never would do something often state that they began with a curiosity regarding pornography. They have admitted that pornography had a high influence on the crimes they committed.

The key point is this: Men, don't deceive yourself! Don't think that it's going to just stop at one of these stages and will never move beyond that. There is a reason you are reading a book on overcoming an addiction to pornography. There is a reason that marriages are destroyed—it's because a man acted out in some way. The risks are huge. The rewards are *zero*.

Points to Consider

1. What stage are you at?
2. How far are you into your addiction? Is acting out the next step?
3. What risk is there? What are you going to do to get help? At this stage, you need professional counsel to help you stop your addiction, because you will not be able to stop on your own.
4. Have you acted out? If so, in what ways? (Even if it has been in subtle, nondescript ways you believe are illegal, you need to be aware that you are acting out.)

6. Scripture Reading: Mark 7: 21-22; Colossians 3:5

Unique Addiction

Sexual addictions are unique because they directly affect the soul. According to the Bible, when we sin against our own bodies, it affects our minds as well as our whole selves. There can be alcohol addictions or gambling and smoking addictions—literally the list is endless for the types of things people can find themselves being controlled by.

However, a sexual addiction is unique. It also is the one addiction that can kick in endorphins. Having an orgasm is a climactic experience, and the mind enjoys what that feels like. Consequently, people who are sexually addicted are, I believe, more deeply addicted; therefore, the addiction is much more difficult to break.

We are sexual beings by nature, and we want to have the comfort and reassurance that a sexual relationship or activity brings. Therefore, there is a direct need. There also is a hormonal need in men and women, especially men, to have that release of energy in order to have that release of feelings. Therefore, sexual addictions are unique and very difficult.

This all means that those with sexual addictions require special treatment. The treatment is more than just talking about it; it's more than just stopping. It is the spiritual element that must be taken into consideration. God needs to be part of the equation. The person addicted needs to ask God to refocus the addiction into things that are healthy. "Help me to stop what I am doing that is so negative and destructive." This reinforces the theme of this book to encourage the building of healthy relationships, healthy marriages. By doing so the person would not need the addiction to supplement or fulfill that desire and craving that God has placed in us.

The endorphins and adrenaline that are achieved through involvement with pornography need to be replaced with healthy methods, such as exercise, stimulating thinking, an adventure (maybe even skydiving)...things that would make your brain and yourself feel better, things that affirm that you do not need to engage in this addiction in order to feel better. Sometimes people who are depressed due to the addiction or other things happening in their lives will use pornography and masturbation to help relieve the symptoms of depression. The problem is that it only makes the depression deeper; it only makes your life emptier and more guilt-ridden.

Points to Consider

1. Are you addicted to the endorphins and adrenaline produced by engaging in pornography and inappropriate activities? Are you using pornography to kick in the rush of these brain chemicals and the pleasure they produce?
2. How do you think that a sexual addiction is different from other addictions? (Specifically as this pertains to you.)
3. What substitutes could you use for your addiction that would be healthy and a better choice?

7. Scripture Reading: 1 Corinthians 6:15-20

North Pacific Plywood Lunchroom

"Tad" was eighteen years old when he got a summer job working for his future father-in-law, who was part owner of a local lumberyard. This teen was greener than green in many areas of life. During the summer of 1969, he learned the seamier ways of the world.

Some real characters worked at the lumberyard. Most were nice guys, but they were a bit rough around the edges and had far different life experiences and perspectives than Tad. The work was hard, manual labor, but Tad persevered and grew stronger over the months.

However, the most challenging part of Tad's day was lunchtime. He could ignore the bad language and the off-color jokes, but the lunchroom itself was just too much for him to handle. Located in a separate, small building, the lunchroom was wallpapered with pictures from girlie magazines. Not just one or two scattered about, but literally the walls, ceilings, and even the benches were covered with the photographs—a full history of *Playboy* centerfolds in chronological order. This was overwhelming for an innocent boy's eyes to behold.

Tad determined he could not eat in that lunchroom, so he took his sandwich and ate outside nearly every day that summer. Filling up on pornography was a path Tad chose not to take. His fellow workers teased him, but Tad knew he was making the right choice.

Back then it was not only acceptable to have pictures like these displayed in the workplace, it was considered part of being in a man's world. In this type of environment, men frequently flaunted images that were not respectful of women. Unfortunately, this was a benchmark period in American society where the acceptance of pornography took root and allowed it to proliferate. It was obvious from the images in the lunchroom that as the months and years progressed, so did the level of nudity and lewdness. Today such displays are illegal because there are sexual harassment laws that address public exploitation of women.

How each of you got started is critical to acknowledge. There is a root cause that needs to be addressed. It has to be rebuked. It has to be forgiven. It can no longer be a secret that you have kept hidden for so many years.

Points to Consider

1.   How did I get started?
2.   What small influences were guised under thinking: It's a man's world; I'm acting like a real man; it's a man's thing to do; it's OK? Unfortunately, all along it was polluting your mind.
3.   In your formative years, what male influences were you fascinated with because they were not the good church boys—they were the "bad" boys you wanted to be like? What behaviors tantalized you and made you want to emulate them? What was it about their interests that hooked you without your even being aware of it?

8. Scripture Reading: Isaiah 44:9

THE LIE OF DECEPTION

In general, when men are initially exposed to pornography, the lie that is formulated and perpetrated is this: "I'm just curious; I just want to see what the pictures look like; I found this site on the Internet and scrolled through the pages; I didn't want to look like a nerd to my buddies; I wanted to fit in with the rest of the guys; I think it's kind of exciting; I just want to know what it's all about."

I think of one young man who got into using pornography without even thinking of the consequences. It was available, and he liked looking at it because it was fun. He was naïve, and it didn't occur to him that this was wrong. Another teen whom I counseled thought he would be accepted if he brought some pornographic images depicting a well-known cartoon character that someone had drawn engaging in graphic activities. He decided that taking these to school would be a way to show he was cool and maybe help him be accepted. When the other students saw the drawings, the school bully threatened to beat up the teen if he didn't go home and print out another set. When the bully was presented with the printouts the next morning in the school hallway, the vice principal caught the youths. They were busted, and their parents became involved in the incident. That teen learned a valuable life lesson.

The lie of pornography comes in various forms. Thinking that your involvement will make you more accepted or will teach you important techniques is the hook that drags you into the addiction. What you soon find, however, is that you need more and more. The disturbing thing about this process is that it is subtle, carefully crafted by the "evil one," which can cause any person to stumble without knowing they have fallen.

Points to Consider

1. What was the first hook that introduced you to pornography?
2. What could have stopped you from doing it?
3. What lie did you tell yourself that it was no big deal?

9. Scripture Reading: Colossians 3:5

ISOLATION

I find that, for many men, pornography is an isolated sin. You hide the material; you hide the sin. You don't talk about it; you don't share it with any friends, your spouse, or anybody. It is your secret war. It's a well-guarded secret that eats at you from the inside out. So the magazines are perhaps hidden in the toolbox on the truck or out in the garage. The videotapes are locked up or stashed somewhere out of sight. These materials are brought out only when your wife or girlfriend is out of the house—working late, at the store, or away for the weekend at her mother's. Maybe you get up in the middle of the night to troll the Internet so no one knows what you are doing.

Pornography is an isolating sin. Yes, men will sometimes talk about pornography when they are joking in a group or talking with their best friend, but it is still considered hush-hush. I encourage you to bring it out in the open. Get professional help. Admit that it is a problem and is plaguing you. Put some things in place to help so that you don't feel alone. I believe that Satan wants you to be isolated because you are more vulnerable, you can rationalize it more, and you can hide behind the wall of secrets and lies that you have built.

The use of pornography can often emerge from feelings of loneliness and isolation. Men use it to fill a void. "I don't have a girlfriend or wife." "My relationship with my wife isn't fulfilling." "I'm not what I want to be." So you go to pornography to live in a fantasy world, which perpetuates the isolation. Once you are into pornography, you become more isolated because of the guilt, the taboo, or the social embarrassment. You may even feel exhilarated because, like a little boy, you think you are "getting away with something" and only you will know about it. Some men even hold back on revealing the addiction because they fear it will affect their career or their Christian status in the community or how their family feels about them. This feeds the vicious cycle of isolation. Isolation breeds more isolation. There is a saying in AA that is very good: Your addiction is only as great as your deepest secret.

How secret is your addiction?

Points to Consider

1. Are you isolated?
2. What are you going to do about the isolation and with whom are you going to talk first?
3. Are you willing to take the step to admit, "I am in pain; I cannot beat this addiction myself?" Remember: Isolation tricks you into thinking you can overcome the addiction yourself, only to make it worse.
4. Do you have any godly male friends with whom you can attend sporting events, get a cup of coffee, play golf, or go to the movies—something healthy and fun?

10. Scripture Reading: Ephesians 4:15-19

STOP KIDDING YOURSELF!

Rationalization is the game we play with ourselves to justify a decision. We engage in it on a variety of levels and subjects. Most of us have the ability to rationalize just about anything—from not going to work to avoiding our addiction to buying something to making decisions. It helps us evaluate what matters most to us—good or bad—regarding our time, our family, and our finances.

But if you are rationalizing about your addiction to pornography, you are engaged in a game of deceit. Over the years I think I have heard every possible excuse and attempt to rationalize a behavior. Which ones do you use? "It doesn't hurt anyone." "This is my personal business." "No one needs to know." "I am not going to get a disease." "I work hard and deserve some pleasure." "My sex life is not fulfilling, so this helps me." "She doesn't understand." "I have learned a lot from watching the videos." "It relaxes me." "It's legal and I'm an adult." "I can't help it." "My dad got me started." "I can stop at any time." "It is not that serious; you are making more of it than necessary."

The list is endless. The problem is that they are all lies. As long as you hold onto these vain attempts to rationalize your involvement with pornography, you will not be able to face the problem for what it truly is—an addiction that controls you and haunts you every day.

Stop kidding yourself! Look yourself honestly in the mirror and start making steps to drop the excuses and move toward full recovery.

Points to Consider

1. What are your excuses?
2. When are you going to face the problem?
3. What are you going to do about it?

11. Scripture Reading: Isaiah 55:7

INVENTORY:
STOP KIDDING YOURSELF!

The purpose of this inventory is to help examine the things you have been telling yourself in order to justify your addiction. Your "yes" responses will identify those subject areas that need to be addressed during your recovery and/or therapy process.

How many of these statements have you used to rationalize using pornography?

I have said the following to myself or to others:	YES	NO
I have a good marriage—we have a healthy sex life; this is just for fun.		
I can leave it alone whenever I want to—it's not that big a deal.		
It's totally private—no one knows about it.		
I don't have to pay for it; it's not costing my family anything.		
Every man does a little of this.		
My wife doesn't meet my needs; she's not available when I need her.		
I work very hard, and I deserve to do this… it's the way I relax.		
My wife would be very uncomfortable with the kind of sex I like.		
Pornography provides "safe sex"—no diseases.		

I'm not a pedophile or pervert—I'm not hurting anyone or doing anything illegal.		
I use it as education so that I am a better lover.		
It takes the pressure off my wife when she's tired or unavailable.		

The Triggers That Got You Hooked

M any things can trigger a person to be attracted to pornography. Sometimes it's loneliness or the lack of healthy relationships. It could be a sense of not being loved by anyone or perhaps not even loving yourself. It may be triggered by anger—something deep down inside that tells you that you deserve more; I want something I can't have.

Men often identify stress as the trigger that pushed them into their addiction to pornography; they see it as a form of release from the pressures of their job or their life or financial concerns. Many triggers, if not recognized and avoided, could lead men into using pornography.

Knowing what your triggers are—what the driving force is behind your addiction—and then knowing what you are trying to escape from through pornography is part of the cure.

Points to Consider

1. What was the primary cause of your attraction to pornography? Was it loneliness, anger, or stress?
2. Do you remember when the triggers became evident?
3. What is the one trigger that keeps pushing you further and further into your addiction?

12. Scripture Reading: 2 Corinthians 10:5

PHONE SEX

C alls to illicit numbers or to "900" area codes on their phone bills—these are things that men addicted to pornography do not want anyone else to find. Phone sex is advertised in various publications as well as on videos and television. The lure is the belief that you are going to be talking with someone and you can share your fantasies "live."

The reality is that you are probably talking with someone in another part of the country or the world who is working for minimum wage at a phone bank. She doesn't know you, and she doesn't care about you. She'll say whatever you want her to say in order to keep you on the line for as long as possible—that's how they make money.

I had a patient who admitted to me that in one month he had run up more than $600 in charges for phone sex. Once you become addicted to this particular form of pornography, you can never get enough of it. Furthermore, there are some "tricks of the trade." The phone sex vendor may give you the first few minutes for free or a low cost, but then you pay a higher rate for the subsequent minutes. They know that the caller is becoming aroused, and they want to keep him on the phone for as long as possible. Their gimmick is to keep those minutes ticking. And men continually fall for it. These guys believe this is something real. What a lie!

Points to Consider

1. Have you ever tried phone sex?
2. What did you feel when you were doing it?
3. Have you quit? Are you willing to stop? If you have stopped, what made you quit?

13. Scripture Reading: Hebrews 4:12-13

GENERATIONAL SIN

Generational sin has biblical roots in that it means the sins of our forefathers have been passed along to subsequent generations. There is debate on whether or not these are learned behaviors or if they may be genetic or if it is perhaps a spiritual issue. No matter, the sin is passed on. Alcoholism and other addictions show up in generation after generation in some families. "My grandfather drank, my dad drank, and I learned to drink from them. Don't all men drink to prove they are men?"

Pornography is oftentimes generational. It's a spiritual oppression that passes from father to son or uncle to nephew. Whatever the source, it is implied that the activity is normal and acceptable. You might hear a man say, "My grandfather used to have girlie magazines in the bathroom. Nobody said anything, and it didn't seem to bother Grandma. So who cares if a guy looks at these pictures? When we got the Internet in the house, I began looking at Web sites. Nobody seemed to notice. So what's the problem?" Have you found yourself thinking or saying any of these phrases?

So what *is* the problem? It's that the moral fiber of the family is raveling, literally coming apart at the seams. The virtues of purity and fidelity and cherishing women have been compromised or are absent. Healthy relationships are not valued or role models for them don't exist. Addictive behaviors have been rationalized into acceptance.

It is important to note that generational sins are not dependent on or a reflection of economic or social status or church status. It is well known that children who come from both impoverished and wealthy families are susceptible to many addictions. Even though a home and family may look good on the outside, it doesn't mean there is not corruption or pornography taking place that is destroying the lives of those people.

Generational sins can be broken only through repentance. A confession that the addiction is wrong and a change in behavior must occur. A man must make a commitment to stop the activities, and the family must say that they will no longer tolerate the behavior. Generational sins are very difficult to break, but with the help of the Holy Spirit and through the power of God, as well as effective counseling, these sins can be broken, thereby freeing sons, grandsons, and great-grandsons from carrying the burden of generational sin.

If you are the originator of this addiction in your family, stop now to ensure that future generations are not affected. If you are someone who "inherited" this sin, break the chain now. I believe you have the strength and courage to do it.

Points to Consider

1. Is your sin generational? Is it possible that you don't even know it, but it has impacted you spiritually at a subconscious level?
2. If it is generational, are you willing to break the chain right now?
3. How are you going to stop the generational sin so that your own children do not carry the burden of generational addiction?

14. Scripture Reading: Numbers 14:18; Matthew 18:6

SHAME

Shame could be viewed as someone feeling like the broken Christmas toy that no one else wants. Many men feel a deep shame, and that oftentimes becomes the impetus or energy that drives them into pornography. They feel shame that they are not the men they wish they could be and that they are not as successful as they were supposed to be according to their parents or their own expectations. Perhaps they feel shame due to their sexual performance or the size of their genitalia or the way they relate to women. Maybe they are unsure how to please women emotionally or socially.

They experience a sense of loss and believe they are not the men they ought to be. So they choose to create this fantasy world of pornography that only feeds the shame even more. It gives the illusion that "Now I'm going to be a big man. I will be young again. I'm going to have strong muscles. I can perform in amazing ways." But when it's all over, there is great emptiness that seems like a lone feather blowing across the vast sea. Furthermore, the man then feels even more emasculated and less of a man. The shame takes a deeper hold, developing into a cycle of being lost, wanting to be fulfilled, going to the pornography, being disappointed, experiencing more shame, and even more loss. The cycle goes around and around. Breaking it is critical.

I encourage you to examine your shame and its source. The fact that you feel like a loser is not from the Lord. Those are feelings you have adopted because you have been in an abusive situation, you have developed this belief yourself based on life experiences of self-talk, or perhaps you have been oppressed by the devil himself. You are a child of God. You are complete. You are unique. And you will be free.

Points to Consider

1. How much shame do you feel and in what areas?
2. In what part of the cycle do you constantly feel trapped?
3. From which part of the cycle do you feel you could most easily break free?

15. Scripture Reading: Isaiah 54:4a

SEXUAL ABUSE

O ne of the things we know about people who have gotten into pornography is that they were exposed to it by a father, an uncle, or a brother, or they were abused themselves.

Sexual abuse is tragic. It changes people's lives permanently. For men, especially, it's a violation. It's almost indescribable. This is especially so if there has been penetration or severe molestation or repeated events in childhood and early developmental years.

Abuse distorts an adult's sexuality. They therefore see that pornography is nothing more than an extension of that very world they were exposed to. They do not sense that it is wrong or that it is dirty or that it is inappropriate because they themselves have already been violated and feel broken. Being broken is one of the critical parts of pornography use and the addiction. It's knowing that you are different, that you are less than normal. Sexual abuse also takes away one's self-esteem, one's identity, one's privacy. And the very essence of what they want to give that is pure and clean they feel shameful about. They feel that they are a broken toy that no one wants.

Sexual abuse can be stopped. The key issues are to: 1) get some help; find someone with whom you can talk openly about it—you must get the pain out; 2) be around people who know what healthy sexuality is, reading healthy books not pornographic or lewd materials. Surround yourself with what is normal, what is healthy, what is acceptable. Look for the parts of the human being that are emotional, that are touched by the heart and not just by the physical or by the attraction of the sex act itself.

Sometimes when people have been abused, they use that as an excuse. They say that's the way it's always been; that's the way I am; I can't help it. I'm the victim. You must stop the victimization issue. You must not use it as a crutch. You have to address this issue and say: "Yes, I have been violated, but that does not give me the excuse or the reason to continue to violate myself or my spouse by engaging in pornography and perpetuating the very thing I hate."

Points to Consider

1. Were you abused? If so, acknowledge that it occurred and to what extent.
2. What are you going to do to get the pain out and relieve it?
3. What would healthy sexuality look like and how would you implement it?

16. Scripture Reading: Psalm 59:1-4

SINGLES

I n today's society it is fairly standard for young singles to wait until their mid-twenties to become engaged and married. In other cultures, a youth goes through puberty and soon gets married. There are societies where having more than one partner is the norm. For example, in some areas of Africa, where the spread of HIV/AIDS is rampant, there are cultures where the man has his "big house," which is the residence of his primary wife, and his "small house," where five or six women live with whom he has sexual relations.

Single people are challenged in Western culture. Where do they go to release their sexual tension in a healthy way? Are they supposed to masturbate? Is that practice acceptable in their theology? What do they do with the natural desire to be with someone—not just to have sex, but to be intimate and close?

Consequently, pornography may become even more appealing to a single person. At least a married person has the possibility of engaging in sexual activity with a partner where there is affection and warmth and a genuine release of tension. Single people are easy targets because they struggle more, and pornography is a temptation to which they can very quickly succumb. These singles believe they can engage in sexual activity without committing adultery or fornication. But pornography is a form of fornication because it is lust, and it is sex. It can even become adulterous in that the addict desires another person's partner. When that happens, the single person has crossed the boundary physically, mentally, and emotionally.

I know that singles are struggling to deal with their sexual nature in our society, especially if they want to remain pure. Talking does help, as can being with people who can support them. Sometimes finding physical activities to channel energies can help as well. But in all honesty, it is a struggle for many, many men because it is a natural desire to want to be sexually active.

The issue of singleness is not just for the young. There are many men and women who are older and are single through a variety of circumstances. Divorce or death may have occurred, or perhaps a spouse is fighting a long-term illness or is unable to engage in sexual activity due to past abuse or trauma. There are times when everyone struggles with sexual tension. Even when married, the opportunity for release and closeness may be lacking. The battle is real and challenging.

I also want to reinforce the fact that though expressing our sexuality is very important, it is merely one part of our total being. We also are intellectual, we have careers, and we have other interests, thoughts, and goals. Perhaps society puts too much emphasis on sexual activity. It is a minor slice of your entire life and who you are. Therefore, let's work toward keeping it in perspective and not overemphasizing that we have to be sexually active to be complete. You are complete, even if you must remain celibate for a period of time.

Points to Consider

1. Are you single? Do you struggle?
2. Where can you put your energies that is healthy?
3. As a single person, how should I handle my sexual nature?

17. Scripture Reading: 1 Corinthians 7:8-9

FEAR OF REJECTION

One of the reasons men like pornography is because they can control the types of images, they can fast forward or rewind the tape, they can select their preferred Web sites, they can buy their favorite magazine, and they can call the 900 telephone numbers that offer the most appealing voices. There is the sense that "no one can reject me." "The images don't talk back to me; they don't know me; they don't reject me for any physical, mental, or emotional reasons. And, most important, it's there when *I* want it."

The fear of rejection is authentic in the real world because you are aware of the following: "*I* have to engage in a live conversation, *I* have to make a commitment, *I* have to be thoughtful, *I* have to step up to the plate and reveal my true self." In pornography the fear of rejection is removed, thereby giving it more of an attraction and, consequently, making the addiction even more complicated.

All of us experience a fear of rejection. All of us feel we are inadequate in certain areas: sports, music, public speaking, mathematics, technology, business...the list is endless. The fear of rejection is not all bad. It helps us learn to overcome our fears. By stretching and challenging us, we grow. However, when we shift that fear into the context of an addiction to pornography, a healthy fear becomes distorted and feeds on itself. The fear of rejection is never resolved; it fact, it only grows.

Each of us has experienced some level or form of rejection. In my early practice I had a patient who felt he was a wimp. He went to great lengths to build up his body. This man became quite muscular and attractive. One day he met a woman and decided to take her to a room on the top story of a five-story hotel. As he disrobed, she made a very rude comment about his genitalia. He became so distraught that he jumped out of the window. His injuries were not life threatening due to his excellent physical condition, but emotionally he was a wreck. He came to my office and we discussed the situation. In consulting with his medical doctor, it was determined that his genitalia were normal. Despite all the work he had done to develop his body and build his confidence, her comment was like a knife slicing away at his self-esteem.

Everyone needs to have enough sense of self-worth and confidence to say, "Just because someone said or did something to me does not make it true." If you have been rejected once or twice or however many times, it does not mean it will occur for the rest of your life. Each of us has qualities that are enduring and valuable, and those will reap huge benefits in real relationships with real people who understand and love us for who we are.

Points to Consider

1. What fears of rejection do you have?
2. What can you do or learn or practice to build your confidence?
3. How do you use pornography to make yourself feel accepted and not rejected?

18. Scripture Reading: Psalm 35:1-4

CHAPTER 2

THE EFFECT ON SELF, WOMEN, AND OTHERS

"Martin," a civil engineer with a successful career in local government, stays up all night trolling the Internet to find the most graphic material possible. Now 37, Martin has been a regular user of pornography since the age of 19. He goes on line three to four times a week and masturbates while poring over the images. He has abused himself to the extent that he is causing physical damage to his body—not to mention the effects on his mind and soul. He is obsessed and loses track of the time he sits at the computer. His addiction has reached the point where he is missing work due to lack of sleep. Martin is at risk of losing his job, his marriage, and his health.

"Angela," a 35-year-old schoolteacher, has not stopped sobbing since she entered my office. Her husband's hobby of looking at pornography on the Internet has been discovered—not just by her but by their 13-year-old son as well. With tears streaming down her face, she asks me: "How could Martin do this to me

and to our family? Our life is so normal; we both have jobs; we go to church; we love each other and have sex regularly. I'm no prude, but I know that this is unhealthy. What did I do wrong? What if our parents find out? What should I say to my son?"

WHY DIDN'T I SEE IT COMING?

This is a classic question I hear when I counsel people. All addictions have a uniform pattern of progression. What starts as a simple curiosity while in college or the military grew unattended. Why didn't you see it coming? Because the nature of addictions is to blind you. You don't realize that it creeps up on you inch by inch.

The person who receives a DUI conviction will often say, "I didn't realize I drank that much. I didn't think I was that drunk. But officer, I only…" The employee who gets caught with his pornography at work asks, "Why was I so stupid? I knew my job would be at risk. I knew they had filters on the system."

Men have come into my office and shared: "My wife wants me to move out of our family home immediately. She is so disgusted by what she has learned about me and that I have lied to her for so long. Why didn't I see it coming?"

Because you didn't hear. You didn't believe. You didn't see your addiction to pornography for what it really is. You were deaf and blind, and you pretended that the addiction did not exist. Please wake up! You can be assured that "it's" coming—the day you are caught by your wife, your child, or your employer. Just like an infection left unattended will cause future illness or even death, the disease of your addiction to pornography will cause incredible pain and loss. Do not submit your good sense to the lie that "it's not going to hurt me, I'm going to be OK, or I'm the exception." All of us are at risk when we ignore that which we know is wrong and believe it doesn't have any power or consequence in our lives.

Points to Consider

1. You know it's coming...what is it?
2. Are you being blind and deaf to what the reality and consequences of your behavior could be?
3. If you were to overcome the addiction, what could you look forward to doing or accomplishing that would be more fulfilling than what you found in pornography?

19. Scripture Reading: Isaiah 44:9

THE RISK OF BEING CAUGHT/ THE RISK OF NOT BEING CAUGHT

What a dilemma! On one hand you hide, sneak around, make sure no one in the book or video store sees you, and use passwords on the computer and erase the history section. Whatever your game may be, there are risks of being caught. By whom? Your wife? Your kids? What about your employer? Many companies have sophisticated screening for computer e-mails, software, and the Internet. I had one patient employed at a major corporation who was viewing pornography on the Internet six hours a day! This executive thought he was above the radar, so he believed he would never be caught. Well, his use of company equipment to feed his addiction to pornography was discovered; he was put on probation and was required to enter into counseling. This man was very lucky; because of his position with the company, he was able to keep his job.

But what did it cost him? His reputation. The trust he once had known from his employer and his spouse. It cost him his marriage. The price was steep. Eventually everyone is caught.

The Bible says that no sin will go unpunished. The serpent *does* come out from under the rock. Truth will prevail. Some men want to get caught. Perhaps the executive noted above *did* want his secret revealed and that someone would hold him accountable for his actions and offer the help he desperately needed.

So to be caught or to not be caught is a game addicts play in their heads. Part of you wants to be truthful, and part of you wants to keep the secret hidden, because you are fearful of others finding out what you did. On one occasion a pastor came into my office; he was very concerned about privacy and confidentiality. Once assured, he confessed that he had been addicted to pornography for years. Did he want to be caught? No. His career was on the line. And yet he wanted to know there was help for him and that someone cared enough to say, "We can support you and help you get over this addiction."

The ramifications of not being caught are obvious—deeper and deeper progression into the addiction. Months become years; years become decades. Decades become a lifestyle. If you have not been caught, what are the advantages? That you tricked yourself for all these years? That you have gotten more into the addiction? That it takes more to be stimulated? That the relationships that are real have become thinner and more strained? That you are separated from your spouse and family...and God? Remember, the addiction to pornography is a life based on a lie. Not being caught *is being caught* by the web, the bondage, the sin. Be honest with yourself.

Points to Consider
1. What is your inner desire? Do you really want help?
2. What game are you playing to ensure you don't get caught?
3. Whom are you kidding? Yourself? Others?

20. Scripture Reading: Romans 1:21-27

HOW PORNOGRAPHY CHANGES YOU

Why is this sin so different from other sins? Pornography has the ability to alter your moral compass. It makes you see yourself, women, sexuality, society, morals, values, and spiritual beliefs from a compromised position. You have changed the very standards in which you believed. You have now compromised what you once considered moral and right. Your addiction changed you. Therefore, you now look at things through a different set of lenses that are tinted. Your moral compass has been readjusted to accommodate your justification of the habit and to meet your needs. It is not true.

The thing you have to do is to get back on track. Where is the compass off? Where have you altered your thinking and said, "It's OK; it's not a big deal. I'm all right. Nobody knows."

Who are you kidding? What is the reality? And where are your standards? Readjust the standards to fit God's standards and what you down deep really believe is important to you. Stop compromising and stop excusing yourself.

There are also physiological changes when pornography takes priority in your life. For example, the average couple will make love about two or three times a week—given children, busy schedules, menstrual periods...life. I find that men who are addicted to pornography will often masturbate every day. In one case, a male patient would masturbate up to six or seven times each day. This caused him physical problems.

You need to look at the source of stimulation in your life. Is it from a genuine relationship that is based on romance, love, and caring? Or is it based merely on sexual gratification for the simple pleasure of ejaculation or climax? Therefore, where is the distortion occurring? It is not natural for a man to have sex more than once or twice a day. It is also not in God's design to engage in sexual activity without a spouse. This is just total self-gratification, self-satisfaction, and a misperception of what God intended physical relationships and pleasure to mean.

Points to Consider

1. How has pornography changed your moral compass? How has it changed what is true?
2. What are your real standards? What have you compromised and what do you want to change?
3. Are you being true to your spouse, or are you simply gratifying yourself in a selfish manner?

21. Scripture Reading: 1 Corinthians 6:15-20

THE ADDICTION REQUIRES
MORE AND MORE

All addictions require more and more stimuli to attain the desired effect. Smokers don't start out smoking two packs a day. They build up to that level over time. Gamblers start with one bet. Those addicted to power started with their first position of authority. The love and hoarding of money began with not sharing. The same is true with pornography. What excited you sexually when you began using pornography is most likely boring and blah to you now. To get the level of excitement they need, men will seek more graphic, explicit, and lewd materials so they can become aroused and climax.

Addictions are progressive, and even if they are put aside for a time, the person will pick up right where he left off. For example, if a one-pack-a-day smoker quits for a time, when he resumes the habit he will be back at one pack in no time—and will most likely advance to two packs a day. With any habit, you cannot go back to the beginning stages and go through the initial steps again. The addiction controls the need to get to the point of destruction. That is the only expected and logical outcome of an addiction.

The addiction requires more and more, because what was once tantalizing is no longer enough. You now need to go deeper and deeper into the types of materials—maybe even more graphic or to images of children or animals or to sadism or masochism. The endless degree to which some men will go creates greater isolation.

Part of the effect it has on you and the people around you is that you are taking away from them. Whether it is the sleep you miss while engaged in activities you prefer to keep secret, the time you spend with your family, the sexual intimacy you are taking away from your wife, or the honesty—being truthful and realistic with her.

Take an inventory of the effects this addiction is having on your relationship. Is there open and honest communication with your wife? What else are you hiding that also needs to be revealed? If you think that using pornography affects only you, you are lying to yourself. It doesn't affect only you—it affects all the people around you. The closer you become to pornography, the greater the distance you are building between yourself and your wife and family.

By requiring more and more, the addiction also takes more and more away from those people around you. It erodes the very hearts of your relationships. It is truly a roaring lion seeking whom it may devour.

Points to Consider

1. What level is your behavior?
2. How deep are you into this?
3. How many hours a day, how many days a week? How graphic is the material you need to become aroused?
4. What is the outcome of my choice to use pornography?

22. *Scripture Reading: Ephesians 4:15-19*

ANXIETY

A nxiety is knowing and feeling anxious about something we want to either stop or we are afraid might hurt us. Perhaps it is something that could cause us grief. Anxiety presents itself in many forms. Some people experience anxiety attacks with physical evidence. Those who suffer anxiety on a clinical level oftentimes take medication or undergo treatment to learn coping mechanisms.

Anxiety can manifest itself through a tight chest, sweaty palms, headaches, problems with digestion or elimination, sexual functioning, or aches in muscles. It comes in a variety of forms and is very real for many people. Some people learn to cope with their anxiety by using alcohol, drugs, or other addictions, such as pornography. Unfortunately, this reinforces the cycle of anxiety: you feel anxious so you go to your addiction; practicing your addiction only increases your anxiety.

One of the things we know pornography can cause is anxiety. This is primarily because of the guilt it induces. Anxiety is generated through the fear of being caught, the fear of being involved in something that could cause us more pain in our relationship or undermine our reputation. It can rob you of the joy of life; it lowers productivity; it can block you from being creative; it can cause confusion. It can steal the very essence of why we are here in this life. When you are overwhelmed by anxiety, you will not experience peace and joy as well as many elements of your life.

On the positive side, anxiety can actually be a healthy thing because it is an early-warning sign that says: "Stop! Don't do this. Engage in something different."

Rid yourself of the pornography and the anxiety will diminish. The quality of your life will improve dramatically.

Points to Consider
1. Do I have anxiety?
2. What does it look like and how does it manifest itself?
3. How desperate am I to reduce my anxiety? Is it to the point where I am ready to get rid of the pornography?

23. Scripture Reading: Deuteronomy 28:65-67

DEGRADATION OF SELF, WOMEN, AND SEX

One of the most disturbing things about pornography is that it is totally degrading of the woman. The female is put into a very submissive, very subservient, and, sometimes, almost a very demanding role that is not fulfilling to her, is not mutually respectful, is not kind, is not gentle. She is simply being treated as an object—an object of desire, an object of lust. Consequently, it also puts the man in that same position. Because in the use of pornography, he is no longer showing tenderness or a loving side; he is merely an acting machine fulfilling a movie director's instruction.

It also degrades the very act of sex that God says is to be holy and pure between a husband and wife. It's to be personal and on a very private basis. So the fact that it is "lights, camera, action," undermines that the act of sex be intimate and private. Then you have two people performing as directed in sometimes the most bizarre behaviors and in the most debasing ways. It is not natural for a woman to want to have ejaculate on her face. Or for her to be subjected to filthy language or to be treated like a rag doll just so the person watching the movie or Internet site can achieve sexual arousal on another level. This is not what God intended and is completely degrading in all aspects. There is nothing educational about looking at pornography—that is a lie. If you want educational information, there are appropriate materials, or you can ask your medical doctor or pastor.

The use of pornography is degrading to yourself because you subject yourself to the same fantasies or the same images that are in the materials. Therefore, it makes you feel inadequate or as if you are not a whole person. It also gives you filthy thoughts, which is degrading. It gives you ideas that are not of the Lord, that are not wholesome, that are not pure. This type of thinking can consume your mind—at work or school you are losing focus because when you see a woman, you easily yield to inappropriate thoughts. You are degrading yourself on a holistic basis as what was meant to be a small percentage of your life has grown to occupy the majority of your thoughts and activities. You are out of balance.

Points to Consider

1. Do you truly believe that pornography is degrading to women?

2. How has it changed the way you value women and treat them as whole human beings and not merely as sexual objects?

3. Has the use of pornography made sex more than it is supposed to be for you? Has it gone to a level that is obscene and perverted? Has it evolved into more of a fantasy? Are you asking your partner to do things you know she is not willing to do but you continue to pressure her to do?

24. Scripture Reading: Colossians 3:5-10

EMASCULATION

Emasculation occurs when a man feels stripped of his masculinity. In American society, emasculation is manifested in a number of ways. For example, telling a little boy to sit down and be still or not to fight back or not to cry. Perhaps the boy is told to do things a certain way—and only that way. His authority figures may belittle him and tell him to quit acting like a sissy, thereby conveying that he cannot be a "man's man."

Currently in our society there appear to be very few healthy role models or heroes that young boys want to—or should want to—follow. Unfortunately, many men who hold public positions or who are celebrities have compromised their morals, their values, their behavior, and their beliefs.

What does it look and feel like to be strong and healthy, to have an opinion, to fight for a cause, to stand up for what is right, and to feel that you are not a "Lone Ranger"? The emasculation of men is taking place in the media as well. Men are portrayed as hapless creatures who cannot figure out how to turn on the dishwasher, use the computer, shop for groceries for the family, or many other "simple" daily activities. There is a tremendous undertone that loudly states: "You are incapable. You are inefficient. You are not even needed. In fact, you are a burden."

Consequently, the effect on men is that the messages of emasculation are internalized. To overcome these feelings and beliefs, many men have turned to pornography, which is seen as something that validates and boosts their masculinity and reinstates their ego. Unfortunately, this basis of validation is false. For a while, viewing pornography helps make you feel that you are big, strong, needed, desired, all-powerful, and in control. Yet the lie, including emasculation, comes through the pornography because you again feel inadequate, less than secure, less than a "real man." Remember, what you are seeing on the screen is an illusion.

So what does it mean to be a "real" man today? More important, what does it mean to be a man of God? I think we need to look at history for some good examples. We need to examine the lives of men who are godly and who have stood for principles, beliefs, and causes that had purpose—our nation, children. Things that have value eternally. Things that are of God and are worthwhile. Things for which we can stand up and that portray us as true men of God, men who are strong, courageous, chivalrous, and who have principles and integrity. Things that are honorable and that we want to pass on to our children. If you are a father, ask yourself how you want your own sons to be raised. Are you a role model, a hero, a man's man for your children? What is the legacy you are leaving them?

Points to Consider

1. Are you feeling emasculated? If so, how?
2. What would make you feel like a complete man in a healthy context?
3. Who has emasculated you? Have you bought into how the media has portrayed men?

25. Scripture Reading: Proverbs 11:21-22; Psalm 112:1-6

FEELING INADEQUATE

This is probably one of the biggest issues that comes up in the lie that pornography brings forth. The perception is that you are not good enough. Think about it. They have interviewed and screened hundreds, maybe even thousands, of people who are well-endowed, who are extra pretty, who have well-developed, muscular chests, or who have a longer this or bigger that—whatever will sell. These are simply actors and actresses who fake it.

Technical editors touch up, video enhance, air brush, digitally improve—the tricks are endless. All for what reason? To sell their products. But what you are really buying (subconsciously at first) is that you don't feel like you measure up. The production of pornography is a game, a business. The titillation is what is marketed. However, the product you buy is a lie.

Take a step back and be realistic. Do women really respond the way shown in the videos? Do women really want what is depicted? Do they really like that? Probably not. Are most men that virile? Probably not. So after you have viewed the pornography, there is the thinking that "I wish I was like that. I wish I were that model. I could pretend to be there." But you are not. So you feel inadequate. Not just sexually, but overall as a man. You question your own masculinity. Perhaps you feel inadequate in other areas of performance and interaction as well. You wish you could perform those wonderful acts and get your mate to swoon and moan like the women you see on the videos. Please know that such images are lies and that your use of them as a measure for your own self-worth must stop. Realize what is true and what isn't.

God made you in a perfect way. We are not inadequate. We are adequate in Christ. We are adequate as a whole person, not just an image on a screen portraying exaggerated sexuality.

Points to Consider

1. Is it not true that pornography is a myth and a lie?
2. Why do I buy into that lie, and what is my fascination with it?
3. Are you adequate in Christ? How can you feel like more of a whole person?

26. Scripture Reading: Genesis 1:26-27

IT'S ALL ABOUT ME

The "It's-all-about-me" statement became popular in the late 1990s because it says how selfish and one-sided we have become. People are focused on expressing sentiments such as: "I want to talk and be heard." "This is my right." "I have the right to be right." "It's my life, and I will do what I want." "I have the right to buy what I want to buy, see what I want to see, and do whatever I want to do."

This thinking is in opposition to what the Bible teaches. The Bible says, "It's all about others." There are many stories about serving, giving, and loving, caring about, and sacrificing self for others. The effect pornography has on ourselves, women, and others is that it does make us think all about the "me" inside: *my* gratification, *my* needs, *my* pleasure. *Me, me, me.*

Self-centeredness causes isolation, arrogance, false self-esteem, and false self-reliance. Yet it also makes one lonely. When people think only of themselves, they are missing the opportunity to enjoy, give, and receive from others in a balanced manner.

Individuals who are self-centered show a lack of maturity. This isn't related to age; it's related to the emotional, mental, and psychological maturity that allows people to focus exclusively on themselves. Teenagers will oftentimes go through a phase (similar to that of a two-year-old) wherein they almost always say "no" to nearly every question or request simply because they can. Saying "no" gives them a sense of power and a feeling of peership with their parents or other authority figures.

However, self-awareness and self-centeredness is appropriate and healthy in a two-year-old, and teenagers eventually learn that it is not all about them and they break out of that behavior. But the addiction to pornography perpetuates self-centeredness because the user is in control: you pick and choose, and you don't have to give anything in return. Therein lies the emotional stagnation that occurs that does not allow the user to develop into a mature person who can be involved in true, long-term, and loving relationships.

Points to Consider

1. Am I self-centered?
2. How does pornography feed my "all about me" syndrome?
3. What would it look like to turn around my thinking and become a servant, a giver, and a person who sacrifices for others?

27. Scripture Reading: Galatians 5:19-21

THE COST

One of the saddest things I see among men who have been caught up in the addiction to pornography is the cost. What happened to your peace of mind? The spontaneity you once enjoyed in your marriage? The innocence and joy you used to experience? The romance and closeness with your spouse? The absence of these is the cost you have paid for your addiction to pornography. You have paid a cost to engage in an activity that is lewd, crude, graphic, offensive, and invasive for sexual pleasure. The addiction was of your own choice and design.

Most times we measure the cost of an addiction in the money spent to support the habit. Or we consider the fact that the person has lost a job and means of income. Or the person has spent time in prison. I've covered these in other parts of the book. What I want to address here is the cost to you as a unique creation of God and to your self-image. Can you honestly look at yourself in the mirror and say, "I am proud of myself and my relationships. I am content with my addiction. Every area of my life is in balance and honors God." Probably not.

Now you see the world through a different set of eyes— another perspective seen through tinted glasses that make everything look black and bleak.

Consider the total cost to your life, your relationships, and your soul. Take back what Satan has stolen. Take back what you gave away to the addiction. Go back and rebuild that which has been broken and make it stronger.

Points to Consider

1. If you are honest with yourself, where are the peace, innocence, and joy you once had?
2. What has the addiction cost you in terms of your relationship with your spouse?
3. What has been the cost to your own heart and soul? Have you taken away from who you really are?

28. *Scripture Reading: Isaiah 65:6-7*

THE KIDS

The effect of pornography on children is horrendous. It steals their innocence. It steals their ability to learn what is right and good. I cannot emphasize strongly enough that pornography is everywhere. It's not just on the Internet. It's in your child's school—a joke in the hallway, a magazine tucked into a locker, a text message on a cell phone. It's also harassment and name calling and labeling that cause damage—sometimes with long-term effects. Pornography distorts children's sexual values and erodes their self-esteem. It undermines their ability to understand, and perhaps even to have, healthy relationships.

Pornography has lowered the moral standard. In your own child's circle of acquaintances, I can guarantee that some of them are practicing a new form of relationship called "friends with benefits." This means that a teen boy and girl are not boyfriend and girlfriend in the traditional sense. They are just friends who happen to have sex. No strings. No commitment. No consequences.

What a horrible lie! How much have we compromised our values—and the lives of our children—to have this taking place in our society? We have taught our children—through our own attitudes and practices—that sex is casual, it's for pleasure, it's for self-gratification, and it doesn't really require commitment. Children are engaging in acts for which they are emotionally and mentally unprepared and incapable of processing what the implications of sexual activity really mean.

Even with the rampant spread of STDs and the extreme emotional trauma these practices inflict on children, we have taught them that sexual activity is no longer a sacred bond between two people. It's not even personal any longer. There is very little value placed on virginity and saving oneself until marriage. We need to shift this thinking so that children are taught that the goal is waiting until they are in love with their partner and have made a marriage commitment before they have sex. Waiting is a precious gift they can gift their spouse.

One of the effects on our children is that they have become calloused. Their thinking is that sex is just something to do, like going to the mall, playing video games, or any other common activity. They see that a large number of their peers are sexually active, it's highly commercialized, and many times sex is portrayed without a personal connection between the participants. At one time, it was considered that females experienced an emotional tie with their sexual partner and that males did not feel this way. Now the game participants are considered equal. "It's alright to have sex; it means nothing. There are no consequences, and I'm not worried about anything. It just means that both of us want to have a pleasurable experience." How sad and shallow.

The effect on our society is going to be very long term. We need to work to reverse the constant bombardment of pornography on not only children, but on adults as well. The lie of pornography has changed personal values and how people define healthy sex. Let's raise the standard and teach our children that sex is an experience based in love and commitment that is meant to be shared between people who are adults.

Points to Consider

1. What effect do you believe pornography has had on children?
2. What effect has it had on your children—in subtle and obvious ways?
3. What risk are we subjecting our children to with pornography being so available and its use being so widespread?

29. Scripture Reading: Matthew 18:6; Proverbs 22:6

WATCH IT WITH HER

This is an excuse I hear all the time. They are going to use it for educational purposes or that it is also going to arouse her and she will then know what he likes and what he enjoys.

Let me be frank. She hates it! She feels degraded; she feels like she is being manipulated into watching it; she's going to be disgusted; she's going to feel like you don't really want to be with her—that you really want to be with the images on the video or pictures or whatever you happen to have.

So do not think that watching it with her is going to make her a better lover or make her more educated in different techniques or whatever. It's all a lie. Do not watch with her. Do not watch it at all. Do not use that as an excuse to continue your addiction. The effect on her is going to be detrimental and destructive, and it will cause you to grow apart rather than bring you together. It will keep the two of you from engaging in genuine lovemaking. The external stimuli that you are aroused by and thinking she will be aroused by will ultimately undermine your relationship.

If you do have an issue regarding your lovemaking, such as it is not as fulfilling as you would like it to be, use words, use communication, talk with her. Excellent books are available that are legitimate tools that are not pornography and are educational. You can find these in Christian bookstores. There also are speakers and therapists, your medical doctor, or even pastors who address this issue. They can help enhance your lovemaking and bring you and your wife closer together. These options are educational and do not contain the lust and debasement of women. Use words to communicate if you want to enhance the physical intimacy in your relationship. Stay on the "clean" track. Don't bring the pornography into your bedroom or into your house.

Simply put: *GET IT OUT OF THE HOUSE!*

Points to Consider

1. What is your rationale for wanting her to watch pornography with you?
2. What did you intend to accomplish? What was your goal?
3. What will be the effect on her and repercussions on your relationship?

30. Scripture Reading: 1 Corinthians 7:3-5

WHY IS SHE SO HURT?

When your wife finds out about your involvement in pornography, it is devastating to her. She is deeply hurt. She has been violated in a grievous way. You broke the wedding covenant. Your behavior damaged the bond of trust between the two of you.

In order for your relationship to heal, you must take responsibly for your own behaviors. You cannot blame her, or stress, or your job, or your finances—or use any other excuse. Face the sin straight on, and do not lie about what it has done to you and your family. Even if you or your wife act like the effects are minimal, you have to realize that her pain is deep and real. Do not underestimate the damage your addiction is doing to your spouse.

Women immediately blame themselves. They say things to themselves like: I'm not adequate to meet his needs. I'm not pretty enough. I'm not as available as he wants me to be.

Oftentimes this is followed by anger. Why didn't he talk to me? How can he think so little of me and our marriage? Can I ever trust him again about anything?

You need to acknowledge and validate her feelings. It is at this point that some couples cannot get beyond the hurt and anger, and the damage leads to separation and divorce. It is imperative that you seek help through a professional Christian counselor who has experience in sexual addiction.

The addiction must be addressed, but rebuilding your relationship is also important. The longer you put it off, the deeper the wound grows. Open and direct discussion needs to take place to restore honesty, trust, and sexual healthiness in your marriage. This process will take time. You must also realize that the addiction may remain an issue for the rest of your relationship. There is hope. When the addiction is put aside and forgiveness has taken place, I have seen relationships become even stronger. But as with anything worthwhile, it takes time and hard work.

Points to Consider
1. Does you wife know about the sin?
2. Are you discussing it with her openly and completely?
3. Are you receiving help in the restoration process?
4. Do you respect her hurt?

31. Scripture Reading: Hebrews 13:4; Colossians 3:19; 1 Peter 3:7

HIS NEEDS, HER NEEDS

There really is a difference between the man and the woman. As you examine Scripture, you note that God displays characteristics that could be considered both male and female. Therefore, men are made in the male image of God, and women are made in the female image of God. They are definitely not the same. Women have different needs than men—emotionally and physically.

Men are hardwired and visually stimulated. Therefore, pornography is predominantly a male issue. Very few women are even remotely aroused by pornography. In fact, the majority of women are disgusted by it. The fact that men think women are aroused by such materials is not true. The real way to arouse and stimulate her is to offer her respect, honor, trust, communication, monogamy, loyalty, caring, romance—all the things that are of the heart.

That doesn't mean that men don't want and need things of the heart as well. It just means that men are hardwired and creatures who are stimulated by visual images. Men look at a woman's body or her face. Every man has a particular part of a woman's body that he finds highly attractive and stimulating to him. Some men prefer to look at breasts, the buttocks, or the legs. This is fine. But this also can be the trigger that leads men into using pornography.

Consequently, men who are programmed to be stimulated by certain images are more easily trapped into the addiction to pornography. In realizing that women's needs are not based so much on physical images, men need to recognize and address their own inner selves to develop their sensitivities and their abilities to care and to nurture their partners and address her emotional needs. Men need to invest time in their partners to get to know them and love them holistically. This makes women feel more safe, protected, and secure in the relationship and, in turn, more responsive to intimacy. It's not all about the physical aspects of the relationship. It's about who you are as a total person and who you are on the inside, not just the outside.

Trust is critical to and the basis for every successful relationship—whether with a neighbor, a friend at church, a colleague at work, or, most of all, your spouse. Ask yourself if there is genuine trust that includes honesty, integrity, and complete openness about yourself and your activities. If you are hiding your involvement with pornography, forget it. She knows it. And it is breaking down any trust in your relationship. She probably is afraid; she does not feel safe; and she feels betrayed. You are no longer meeting her needs or the needs of the relationship.

Points to Consider

1. Are you aware of your partner's inner needs and what she really wants?
2. What are your needs? Have you thought beyond the physical to your innermost needs?
3. Do you talk with your partner about what you each need? Remember, it's OK to communicate about how you feel and what you both need other than the physical. She'll welcome the dialogue, and you both will reap the rewards!

32. Scripture Reading: Genesis 1:26-27; 1 Corinthians 4:2

HUGS—MEETING THE BASIC PHYSICAL NEEDS

Each of us needs touch. Each of us needs hugs. In today's society, many men do not receive hugs. Perhaps this is because they are single or they don't have children or family close to them. It is now inappropriate in the workplace and some social situations to hug unless it is mutually agreed upon. Basically we are in a no-hug, no-touch phase in America today. In some churches or other groups, hugging is encouraged to show that people are welcomed and loved.

The bottom line is that we all need hugs...but we need hugs from healthy people with healthy motives in healthy ways.

Oftentimes when men do not receive the touch they need, they will reach out for other opportunities for engagement. One of these is pornography, which provides a way for men to pretend they are being touched and that they are engaged in an activity that brings them close to another and is real.

Hugs do not need to be sexual. They can simply be a form of affection, friendship, warmth, an expression of appreciation or love. It's OK to give and receive hugs in a healthy way.

Points to Consider
1. Do you receive hugs? From whom? How often?
2. Do hugs create sexual feelings in you or do they generate simply a warm feeling?

3. If you are not receiving healthy hugs, where would be the most likely place to get them?

33. Scripture Reading: Proverbs 3:8

WOMEN'S SIXTH SENSE

Guys, let me tell you something. Every woman who has ever come into my office or that I have ever talked with, including my own wife, automatically is born with a sixth sense. Men know they have the five senses of seeing, hearing, tasting, touching, and smelling. But women have an inner knowledge—intuition. I believe that it comes from the feminine characteristics of God. Trust me, women know. You can try to keep a secret from them, but it will be revealed.

Almost every woman who has been involved with a man addicted to pornography has said to me, "I knew all along. I knew he had magazines. I knew he was on the Internet. I just didn't want to face it. I didn't want to rock the boat. I didn't want to cause trouble in our marriage. But I could tell by his eyes; I could tell by his sexuality. I could tell by the way he talked to me or the things he would ask me to do. Something wasn't right; something wasn't pure. Something was putting a wedge between us, was driving us apart. But I was afraid he would leave me. I was afraid he would be angry. I was just afraid. So for a long time I chose to avoid it, but now I can't. It's gone on too long. It hurts too much. It scares me. Something has to change."

Let me say this loud and clear: *She knows!*

Don't lie to yourself. And don't even try to lie to her. She is not stupid. Remember, you married a smart woman. You married a woman you loved. Don't underestimate her. She knows. Be honest, get some help, and work with her to rebuild your relationship and make it healthy.

Points to Consider

1. Do you admit that she does know something is going on?
2. When are you going to talk with her about your problem?
3. Are you ready to stop lying and start basing your life on truths?

34. Scripture Reading: Proverbs 5:20-23

CHAPTER 3

THE SECRET, THE LIE

Henry has kept his secret so long that he is convinced no one will ever know. He rents a separate post office box in another part of the city where he receives his "special" literature. Near there is his favorite store where he purchases videos. Henry even has a multi-tiered password protection system on his laptop. No one will ever find out about his "hobby." No one...except his wife, his daughters, his in-laws, his pastor, his neighbors, and his coworkers.

Unfortunately, today Henry decided he was no longer satisfied with being a passive participant. He needed to increase the level of physical thrill and satisfaction. So he decided to try something new and exciting. The result? Henry was just arrested for lewd conduct in public—police caught him masturbating in his car during daylight. Given Henry's position in the community, the arrest became an item for the 11 o'clock news. That night pictures appeared on everyone's TV displaying

Henry's humiliated face and his teary wife, Marge, emerging from the city jail.

When the couple went to claim Henry's car, his wife saw the pornographic materials strewn across the seat. In spite of feeling overwhelmed by the immediate situation, many things about Henry and their life together began to make sense to her. Now Marge's intuition is confirmed: Henry is deeply addicted to pornography. The secret is revealed and the truth must be faced.

WHY YOU HIDE IT

Y ou *know* why you hide it! Because you are ashamed. It is a natural response. Even people who say, "Our family is open about this. She understands. I think there is nothing wrong with it. It's perfectly fine."

The question I often ask is this: "If your use of pornography is nothing to be hidden, then let's tell your pastor. Let's bring in your daughter and let her know. What do you think her response will be if she's age 10, 13, 16, or 27? We'll just sit down with a cup of tea and chat; then we'll bring out the magazines, boot up the computer and go to your favorite Web site, or even watch the video on the big screen TV."

To whom are you lying? It's a secret, and you hide it. And you hide it in the most obviously "clever" ways, as if no one really knows what is out in the garage or in the closet underneath your sweaters or under the bed (which is the most obvious place every mother looks). Perhaps you think you've been particularly sneaky by stashing it in the computer under mysterious codenames and behind complicated passwords. You're hiding it because you are ashamed and you know it is wrong.

No matter how well you think you have hidden your addiction, it is still a lie and a secret that takes precious physical and mental energy to try to keep hidden. But the truth is someone already knows or at least suspects. Don't risk a son or daughter finding your secret stash or files. Respect yourself and get rid of that which is hidden.

Points to Consider

1. Where are you hiding it?
2. How clever do you think you are? And how stupid do you think the people around you are?
3. Would you show your daughter these materials if you had to?

35. Scripture Reading: Isaiah 45:16; Daniel 9:8

AFFAIRS WITH PORNOGRAPHY

The Bible describes an affair as anything that separates us from God. People can have an affair with money, an affair with lust, an affair with pride; people can have an affair with anything that breaches our covenant with the Lord.

In our culture, we assume that an affair means a sexual affair with another woman or man. That isn't true. It can be something we hide. Pornography is an affair of lust that is not based in reality. Men lust after what they do not have or what they wish they had. The point is that it separates men from their spouses; it separates them from God because it is a sin. Don't call the addiction to pornography an *issue*—it is a sin. It's real. Addicts are in love with the pornography. They feed their passion; they buy things for their lover. They invest money, time, and energy in the affair. It consumes their lives. The affair with pornography separates husbands from wives. It keeps you from engaging in a real relationship. It is an affair of the mind and of the body. It is an affair that you created and keep alive.

And while you are consumed by the addiction, you are eating upon it. This is almost like a carcass. As ugly and disgusting as it is, you go and feed off the carcass, hoping to find some morsel, only to find that it is rotten.

The affair gives away your heart—the essence of who you are. It's not just the physical elements you have surrendered, it's your very self. When you gave that away, you broke the covenant you made in your marriage. To love, to cherish, to adore. You broke that covenant before her and before

God. Therefore, is your wife angry? Is she jealous? Is she frightened? Is she insecure? Of course she is, because you have done something against what you promised her on your wedding day. You need to go back and heal that and make it right. Don't just say you are sorry; it needs to be a true repentance of the heart that communicates to her that you are loyal only to her and not to the affair.

Points to Consider

1. Do you admit that your involvement with pornography is an affair?
2. How has the addiction separated you from your spouse?
3. Why do you perpetuate the affair and nurture it rather than your relationship with your wife?

36. Scripture Reading: Matthew 15:19; Matthew 5:28

AVOIDANCE

Isn't this the way we muddle through life in so many areas? We avoid facing the fact that we have a problem in a specific area.

Now you are avoiding the issue of your addiction to pornography. You avoid thinking about the consequences. You avoid thinking about the expense of your addiction. Get real. How much money have you spent on pornography? The Internet? DVDs? Magazines? At times you may have cleaned the house of your pornography—only to repurchase the materials. That adds up very quickly to a huge amount of money!

You avoid the reality of what the addiction may mean to your relationship with your spouse, your career, your lifestyle, your children.

Avoidance is a way of denying, and denial is not facing the problem. Be honest. Be sincere. Be truthful. Face what is there. You know it is wrong, and you know the toll the addiction is taking. Quit denying the place you have given pornography in your life and in your heart.

What about intimacy? How many times have you not engaged in a relationship with your wife and met her needs—not just physically but emotionally, but being personal and genuine in your interaction with her? Instead you take the easy route by using pornography to meet your own needs and not hers. Have you avoided your husbandly responsibilities? Have you avoided the genuineness that your spouse deserves and desires? Have you avoided the commitment that you made to her?

Points to Consider

1. How long have you been avoiding the reality of your addiction?

2. When are you going to reveal the addiction and face the reality of its stronghold on your life?

3. When are you going to admit that pornography has a prominent role in your life and has exacted a high price? What is that price?

37. Scripture Reading: Proverbs 6:23-29

DENIAL

D enial is the first stage that everyone will go through. Here is where you say: "I don't have a problem; I have nothing I need to discuss." Again, a secret, a lie. "But I do it only once in a while. I do it only when/because/if…" What's your most common excuse? Denial is not facing the problem; it is not being honest; it is not being real. Denial is a tremendous lie that you are telling yourself.

It's like ignoring the fact that your car needs oil. If you refuse to check the dipstick to see the oil level, then you never "know" that the oil reserve is nearly dry. After all, your car is exceptional—it isn't like other automobiles. You shouldn't need to take it to the shop to find out what is wrong. You can't imagine why the car overheats and you have engine trouble. But then one day the car suddenly stops while you are speeding down the freeway.

Denial does not make any problem go away. In fact, the problem just continues to grow.

We often hear of a person who has not been feeling well but does not seek medical treatment. The pain could be the type that is sudden onset or long-term. The person inherently knows something serious is happening to his body, but he delays seeking medical treatment. When he is finally pushed to go to the doctor, why is he shocked to learn he has a life-threatening illness and his days are numbered?

Denial blocks the reality of a cancer or an addiction growing inside of you. Do not turn your back on the devil, for he will seek and devour your soul. Denial is a trick that allows him to continue to have his way and for the addiction to establish deeper roots within you.

Points to Consider:

1. Are you in the denial stage and continually lying to yourself?
2. How long has the denial been occurring?
3. What is it going to take for you to wake up and face the addiction—and deal with it?

38. Scripture Reading: Colossians 3:9; Ecclesiastes 10:12

IT'S MY FRIEND

This phrase is commonly heard in addiction recovery programs. That friend doesn't talk back; that friend doesn't require me to be responsible; that friend doesn't ask me to sacrifice anything or make a commitment. It's my friend.

Pornography becomes a friend—albeit an evil friend—because you can control everything. You control the remote, the mouse, the page turning, the time and place, the type of material. It becomes your friend—a familiar and comfortable companion when you are tired, stressed, lonely, frightened, anxious. There's my friend. The pictures are always there. I can choose which ones I like, which scenes I like; it makes me feel good and provides a temporary escape from reality, my family, responsibilities, or pain. I can fantasize, relax, masturbate. I can be gratified, and my friend never requires me to stop. My friend doesn't make me feel guilty, and it doesn't ask me to think twice if this is how I want to spend my time. My friend never talks. *It never tells.* So I live a secret lie I share with my friend.

This applies to all addictions—gambling, drugs, alcohol, greed for money, work. Addictions are endless, but they become our friends in a distorted way that destroys and eats. It's a friend that will never call you to accountability. But it's also a friend that does not care about you. It's only concern is the money made from you for the porn industry. This friend does not have you or your family's best interest in mind.

This is an empty friend that steals and lies. You need to recognize that it's not your friend. In fact, it is your enemy. Call it what it really is.

Points to Consider

1. Is it truly a good friend; is it a real, healthy, live friend?
2. What does this friend require of you other than money, time, part of your soul, your self-worth, your sense of value? What price are you paying for this friendship?
3. Is this friend stealing from other areas of your life? Is it taking time from your job or your children, or your wife, or even your own rest?
4. Where is this friend leading you? Is this friend leading you to the kingdom of God and a relationship with him? Or is it separating you from God?
5. How much does this friend care? If you got fired or divorced or your children found out due to your addiction, would that friend be there to pull you out and help things get back on the right track?
6. How many of your real relationships—work, kids, golf buddies—have you abandoned to exclusively be with this friend?

39. Scripture Reading: Deuteronomy 13:6-8

RATIONALIZING

Rationalizing is the ability to justify anything that you want. It is the ability to say, "It's all right, and I am fine. I don't want to talk about it. It's nobody's business but my own."

Rationalizing is a game, a secret, a lie we engage in, and by doing so we can convince ourselves in the most clever, articulate ways. And we believe it! We sell ourselves our own bill of goods because we want to. If we had to say it out loud, how would it sound to someone else? If you were to tape record your mind processing and rationalizing your behavior, would someone else "buy" it? Would you be proud of your thoughts? Or would you want to hide them and keep them secret?

Rationalizing is a clever tactic because a lie can become the truth. And the truth, we believe, will set us free. That's the trap. Because the rationalization is a lie, it is, therefore, not truth and does not set you free. Instead, it traps you in bondage wrapped in a tight and strong hold. Rationalization has to be broken and exposed. The first step is to state your rationale to someone else and listen to how it sounds coming from your mouth. Look at that person's reaction to your "truth." If you can't bring yourself to communicate it to another person, then write it down on a piece of paper. Look at what you said for what it truly is. How do you rationalize what you are doing? What are your reasons? What are your excuses?

Points to Consider

1. Am I rationalizing?
2. What are the reasons and excuses I am using to justify my use of pornography? What is the story behind them?
3. Who is going to believe my reasons and excuses when the addiction is exposed?

40. Scripture Reading: 2 Peter 2:18-19

THE COMMITTEE

T he Committee" is the group of voices in our head that argues with our addiction. Think of it as many people around the table with different opinions. One voice says, "The addiction isn't that bad; you're OK; you can control it." Another voice might say, "You can't control it; it's controlling you." Yet another would say, "I can stop, but I don't want to stop."

Consequently, you have the committee arguing—as Paul says in the book of Romans: "with my flesh and with my spirit"—on the different sides of who you are.

This committee is part of the lie. It's the lie that sends wrong messages and argues about and justifies the addiction. The basic and searching question you must ask yourself is this: Who is the chairman of this committee? It is you, and you have to take responsibility. You need to sort out what lies are driving your addiction. You also need to recognize which things are coming from your conscience and from the Holy Spirit. The Lord does not stop talking to people. People stop listening to the Lord!

Are you hearing things like: This addiction is a secret. This addiction does need to come out into the open, and I need to address it and I need to be honest with myself.

It's time for a reorganization. You need to fire some of the committee members and hire some new people. People who are healthy. The voices you listen to need to be people who lead you to do what is right, who help make you stronger, and who move you in the direction toward healing and overcoming the addiction. Get rid of the negative and lying committee members.

Points to Consider

1. Who is on the committee? Name the different voices and their roles.
2. Who is the chairman, and who or what has the most power? Is it you or is it one of the committee members that is strongest?
3. How are you going to determine which committee members are telling you the truth and which ones are lying?

41. Scripture Reading: Romans 5:19

THE CYCLE

The cycle is a game you play. You buy the magazine or the video. You get sexual satisfaction from the pornography for a period of time. Then you feel guilty and separated from God and your wife. Then you throw the materials in the trash can. Then you go on the Internet and surf to sites where you know you shouldn't go. Then you feel guilty. So you erase the history on your Internet provider. Then you swear to yourself that you are going to stop. You make a deal with God and plead, "Please don't let me get caught. I promise I'll never do this again." Or maybe your wife knows about your use of pornography and you vow to her that you have quit.

But you slip and once again slide into the addiction. You start sneaking to the garage or Web sites where you can feed your addiction. The cycle of addiction can last for years—even decades. The highs and lows—I want to do what I want to do; I feel guilty; I make a deal with God; I make a promise to myself and my wife; I break my promise; and I repeat the cycle.

What are the triggers that cause you to start the cycle over again? Examine your addiction's history and note those times when it has had its strongest hold on your life and when it has been minimized or nonexistent. What kind of relationship do you have with your addiction? Do you love it or do you hate it? When you are not practicing the addiction, do you miss it? Do you feel deprived? What lures you back? Is it loneliness? Is it anger? What are the things that make you want to avoid the addiction and stay off the cycle?

The cycle must be stopped. The way to ensure it is stopped is through accountability. It has to be stopped by admitting: "I know I am caught in a cycle. Now, how do I break it?" You break it by following these steps: 1) identify the cycle itself, and 2) stop playing the game with yourself, with God, and with others. This takes courage and strength, but recognizing that it is a cycle is a huge step in a positive direction.

Points to Consider

1. What part of the cycle are you in? List the different stages.
2. What deals do you make with God and with yourself that you are constantly breaking?
3. What perpetuates the cycle that constantly has you going around and around?
4. What part of the cycle could you break right now—today? At what point can you say: I will break the cycle right here, right now?
5. What are the triggers that start your cycle all over again?

42. Scripture Reading: Romans 7:19-25

TWO SIDES OF ME

Presenting two sides of yourself is another element of the lie. You have your public side: job, church, family, friends. No one would ever suspect you of having pornography. Absolutely not! You are the upstanding citizen. You are a leader in the church. You are the quiet dad no one would ever think of as having an addiction to pornography.

And yet, in the darkness of your own heart—in the middle of the night, alone on your computer, alone with the TV—is the other you. The lustful man who indulges in disgusting fantasies. This side of you may have been drawn deeper into pornography than you ever want to admit. You may be involved in things that are truly grotesque, absurd, bizarre, and debauched.

Then you turn off the TV or computer (after erasing all the site information that would indicate your addiction), hang up the phone from the sex lines, or restash the magazines. Now you can return to your "normal" life by pasting on your nice smile, putting on your dress shirt and tie, combing your hair. Once again you are the perfect model citizen. What a lie!

How long do you think you can perpetuate this myth?

Having two sides of yourself is exhausting. It wears you down physically, emotionally, and intellectually. And even though you may not see it, you may not even believe that the addiction is taking its toll, the involvement with pornography is stealing your life. You cannot be two people.

The Bible teaches us that we cannot serve two masters. Which master are you serving first? Which master is the truth? Which master is real?

Points to Consider:

1. How many sides are there to you? Perhaps there are more than two. What are they?
2. Why do there have to be two sides of you? What are you doing that perpetuates this?
3. What is it going to take to get rid of the side of you that takes away the quality of life you really want and squeezes out other people and healthy activities?

43. Scripture Reading: Luke 16:15

Don't Talk, Don't Feel

Don't talk, don't feel" is a phrase that is used in ACOA (Adult Children of Alcoholics). Children learn from their parents that no one wants to talk about an addiction to alcohol—the monster or, as AA calls it, the elephant—in the living room. Therefore, because you don't talk about it, you don't need to feel it. If you don't feel it, then it doesn't exist.

The same applies to the addiction to pornography. "If I don't talk about my addiction and I categorize it or file it away in my own mind, then I don't need to feel anything. Consequently, I'm off the hook…it doesn't exist. It's not a problem. I don't need to discuss it. I don't need to feel guilty about it. And I certainly don't need to deal with it."

What a lie! What a convenient escape for the secret!

The answer is obvious. Yes, you must talk. Yes, you must feel. You are a real person. The pornography is fake. It's easy for it to be categorized, or as we sometimes label things such as this: minimized and sanitized. You are real. The people in the pornographic materials are real. They have given their bodies for profit. You must emerge from the secret. It's time to talk. It's time to break the lie. It's time to feel.

Points to Consider

1. Have you stopped talking to yourself or anyone else about your addiction?
2. Have you stopped feeling, and at what level?

3. When are you going to open up with what you are
    really feeling and not be afraid? Do you have a trusted
    confidant?

44. Scripture Reading: James 5:16

CONTROL

You know what's nice about pornography? You get to control it. You can control the tape or DVD, the magazine, the telephone sex line, the computer—you can pick anything you find stimulating. Whatever your fetish or passion or desire is, you get to pick from millions of choices of what attracts you. So whatever gets you aroused—legs, shoes, breasts, blondes, redheads—you are totally in control.

What a lie! You are in full egotistic mode. You think that because you can pick whatever you want, this is great because you are in control. And yet, it's not real.

Think about it. You are in control of what? An image you are viewing? The reality is that you are out of control! You have lost control of what is true, genuine, sincere, rewarding, and long term. So you have control of your life, the pictures, and your actions for say twenty or thirty minutes? The idea that you are in control is an illusion. In reality, when it is all over, you are out of control.

Part of the lure of being in control of pornography is that you feel so out of control in other aspects of your life—your job, your family. Maybe you feel you are manipulated, unappreciated, not respected, or were overlooked for a promotion you deserved. Maybe you aren't feeling in control of your children. They no longer respond to your authority and you can't handle them. Maybe your finances are out of control. Or even your marriage. Therefore, you grab on to what you can control. Pornography is "your world" and no one else can invade it. You think, "It is my private world, my sanctuary where I control everything that happens." So even though you can't control society, complex corporations, or even the life you lead with its hectic schedule, you continue to go to that place where you love to hide and where you feel in control—the use of pornography.

The bottom line is that you are never in control of the addiction; the addiction is *always* in control of you.

Points to Consider

1. Who (or what) is truly in control? The media? The system? The addiction?
2. What is the addiction in control of in your life?
3. Are you tired of trying to be in control of your life when you know it is so out of control?

45. Scripture Reading: 1 Thessalonians 4:3-5

GUILT—REAL AND FALSE

Real guilt is caused when you do something wrong: you cheat, you lie, you steal. These result in you feeling guilt—and you should! You pay a penalty; you go to jail. The consequences are real.

False guilt is when you feel guilty for something you didn't do wrong. It is usually perpetuated by a religion or by a family system. So you think, "I ought to feel guilt for what I have done." And yet there is no way to pay the price or to repent.

Let me be very blunt here: Pornography causes real guilt. There is something within your heart, within your soul, something in the pit of your stomach that says, "What am I doing? Why am I doing this?"

Over time, people who have become addicted to pornography come to override the nudging of their heart or their gut. You no longer feel the guilt. You justify and rationalize and begin to accept the behavior. Therefore, it becomes a part of your fabric, a part of your character.

The point is this: Are you guilty of sin? Is the Holy Spirit convicting you that things are out of alignment in your life? Where are your morals? What has happened to your conscience? Where did your values go? Isn't there still a part of you telling yourself, "What I am doing isn't good for me physically or mentally. It isn't good for my family. How can I stop? Why did I get into this habit?"

Once your conscience has been reawakened, admit that you are guilty. Come forward. Ask for forgiveness from the Lord. Ask for forgiveness from your spouse. And accept that you are forgiven. Now is the time that you must change your behavior. You must look at what you are doing and recognize that it is not healthy. Proclaim to yourself: "I want this out of my life!"

When we confess our sin, we are free of it. But we must also stop the very things that feed the sense of guilt: the thoughts, the behavior, the secrecy, the isolation, the lies. Guilt is not of God. God is grace; he is forgiveness. But do not abuse God's grace. There are also consequences for our sins. The Bible says that sometimes the consequence of sin is death. Perhaps not always physical death. But maybe spiritual death, emotional death, relationship death. Be honest with yourself. What price have you paid for this addiction to pornography or even the propensity to like pornography on an occasional basis? Whatever the cost, it is too great.

Let your guilt evolve into resolution and find the strength to commit that you are going to begin on the road to recovery.

Points to Consider:

1. Do you feel guilty?
2. If you don't feel guilty, *why*? What are you continuing to do to justify your addiction?
3. What are you going to do to rid yourself of the guilt and the pain?

46. Scripture Reading: Job 36:8-12

FETISHES

F etishes are things that become sexually attractive through association. For example, she is wearing stiletto heels. So now these long, tall heels or fishnet stockings or a particular bra or long earrings or a specific ethnic group or suggestive language become the source of your arousal. The pornography industry uses the human tendency to associate as a tool of their trade. They create media that focus on whatever your particular touchpoint is. They will insert these elements to draw you into using their product—it's a marketing ploy to get you to buy their DVD, Web site, etc. Another example is thematic programming such as college students on vacation—this is a fetish that features young women at the beach or at parties. You cannot date them in your real life, but you can pretend to have a relationship with them.

This practice merely perpetuates the lie. The fetishes are an association and become a trigger that arouses a memory, a fantasy, a hope. The truth is that these are all just like fishhooks ready to reel you in for "dead bait."

A fetish is something you have come to associate with pleasure. No matter what it is, it triggers an inner switch in your psyche that says, "I like this pleasure. Would you please wear this? Would you please say that to me when we are being intimate?" All of this degrades and dehumanizes your partner for the exclusive purpose of you deriving pleasure. But a fetish always will be nothing more than a fantasy. You need to love and appreciate your spouse for her real attributes, not the ones you imagine or try to impose on her.

Get away from the fetishes. Using them takes you further from reality and sets your relationships up for failure. Are you asking your wife to wear a particular costume or undergarment or lingerie only so that she can help you pretend she is something she is not? You need to look at who she is as a real person, a genuine person inside and outside—someone to respect and cherish for being the unique creation God has blessed you with to share your life. Do not play the game and become so hooked on your fetish that you sacrifice a real and fulfilling relationship. Don't allow yourself to become your own selfish self.

Points to Consider

1. What fetishes are you addicted to?
2. What makes them special?
3. How are you going to break the attraction to that fetish?

47. Scripture Reading: Ezekiel 20:30; Philippians 4:8

MASTURBATION IS SELF-LOVE

This is a very graphic and personal topic. Though it may be considered rather "out there," the subject needs to be addressed sincerely—even within a Christian context.

The act of masturbation is taking yourself into your personal world for your own gratification. It is a real part of life for many men. I believe that most males do masturbate at some point in their life—usually during adolescence. Unfortunately, males who masturbate as adults often have an addiction to pornography. In my practice I have learned that men seem to have a memory bank where they store images, thoughts, jokes, fantasies. The problem is that it is all about you. It's all about what you like or what you believe or what you think or what you want to have. It may even be perverse and something you would never share in public or with a sexual partner.

The underlying problem is that the practice of masturbation isolates you from your spouse—the touch, the relationship, the emotional and spiritual aspects of being with someone. It takes away from a loving relationship wherein you both want to satisfy each other's needs. By masturbating, you are not telling your spouse, "I want to love you; I want to give to you; I want to sacrifice for you; I want to care about you; I want to be with you."

In masturbation you are by yourself—alone with your mind and body, satisfying yourself with your own touch. Everything is all about you. This is very selfish. It means you are not connected; therefore, you are alone. You have

isolated yourself from your spouse and you are being selfish.
Is that what God intended healthy sex to be?

Points to Consider
1. How often do you masturbate? Why?
2. What are you hiding from your spouse?
3. Why is masturbation so important that it has become an integral part of your life along with pornography?

48. Scripture Reading: 1 Corinthians 6:13

PORNOGRAPHY DOES NOT AROUSE WOMEN

How true, how true, how true! "Traditional" pornography arouses men because they are visual. Men are hard-wired and what they see sparks arousal. The assumption that women might become aroused through viewing the same things is a lie. Women are aroused when their emotions and their hearts are touched. Their feelings are kindled when they feel that their husbands love, respect, honor, cherish, communicate, listen to, and protect them. They respond to integrity, gentleness, mutual trust—the qualities and practices that make a woman want to be with her husband in an intimate way.

Women are aroused through gentle touch, through kind words, through romance, and through caring. If you think that watching or sharing pornography with her will spark arousal, you need to realize that in truth it will disgust her. It will *not* be pleasing to her. It will irritate her, it will hurt her, and it will drive a wedge between you. Pornography is not healthy and will not enhance your relationship with your wife. Do not believe the lie that pornography marketers and other users promote. No matter what they say, she is not interested and she will not become aroused. Don't undermine your relationship further by sharing your addiction. Engaging her in looking at the pornography does not diminish your sin or justify your continuation of the practice.

Ask your wife what her needs are. What is it that would make her feel more secure, supported, and loved? How can you improve the connection with your wife? It is not the titillating, physical things that men may think. It is the emotional; it is the sharing and the quality time that you spend with each other. Find out what she needs—*not* just in the bedroom but in her whole life that would make her feel closer to you. By doing these things you will not only build a much stronger relationship, but she will become aroused when appropriate.

Points to Consider

1. Do you believe that women are aroused by pornography?
2. Do you understand what your wife needs emotionally and intellectually—beyond physically?
3. What lie have you been trying to force on her and for what reason?

49. Scripture Reading: Matthew 6:20-23

THE NEW LIE

Creators of pornography are very industrious and clever people. While the male-focused market has been skyrocketing, they have been hard at work producing material to create and capture a new market— women. It is well documented that women are not aroused by traditional pornographic images. However, a whole new genre of videos, books, and Web sites have been engineered to attract women. Statistics reveal that more than fifty percent of women have viewed online adult content.

By addressing the more emotional and relational sexual needs of women, the new pornographic materials geared toward this audience are wrapped in romantic jargon and imagery. The video may start out with a man and woman meeting, striking up a conversation, going out to dinner, and walking in the park. The woman's thoughts may be heard, wondering if there will be a kiss at the end of the evening and if he could be "Mr. Right" and the soul mate she has been waiting for her entire life. Gradually the video changes mood, eventually showing the couple engaged in sexual activity much like what has been included in traditional pornography. The exception may be that the couple cuddles at the end and plans for a long and happy life together.

Don't be deceived: It's nothing but the same old porn wrapped with a pretty pink bow. Unfortunately, its use is on the rise and more women are being lured into the trap. And don't think that you can continue or justify your own addiction if your wife has begun to read or view this type of material. Your addiction already has opened the door for her needs to be met in ways other than what you have been giving to her—or what God intended for your relationship.

The industry's marketing tactics have been successful: it is estimated that between fifteen and twenty percent of all women now struggle with an addiction to pornography. By overcoming your own addiction and getting all the materials out of your house and out of your life, you will be creating an environment where this new attack on your family cannot take root.

Points to Consider

1. Is your wife viewing pornography?
2. If you and your wife are both using pornography, what effect has it had or your relationship?
3. What are you going to do to remove all pornographic materials from your home and ensure that they stay out?

50. Scripture Reading: Galatians 6:1; Psalm 119:133

PORNOGRAPHY IS NOT A TRAINING AID

The publishers and producers of pornography will oftentimes market it as way to educate men on new techniques or to demonstrate the use of a particular adult toy or position that will enhance the ability to make love more effectively. However they package it, the material is still pornography. In fact, viewing such images may be educational in the negative sense in that it causes destruction and perpetuates the lie. It can educate people in the wrong way.

Many good, healthy, and appropriate books are available, as well as therapists who are excellent resources for learning about sex and how to make it fulfilling to couples. You will find that these are not only helpful in a technical sense, but you will develop a greater understanding of how God views the pleasure and holiness of sex between two loving and committed people. Watching other individuals undress, pose provocatively, and engage in pornographic sex is not educational. This is a lie.

Another part of the lie in pornography is that everyone is going to have super wonderful, fantastic sexual experiences and orgasms every time. Pornography is like watching a circus—everyone is doing cartwheels and acrobatics, everyone is shrieking with delight, and everyone is applauded for outstanding performance. This is a huge lie. Therefore, trying to become educated on some "new thing" in hopes that you or she will become even better than your wildest fantasy is not real. It sets you up for disappointment. It creates unrealistic—and unhealthy—expectations. You need healthy education, healthy standards, and healthy information. This will yield healthy relationships.

Many factors affect sexual behavior. We are human beings who have hormones and cycles. For example, a woman's hormones will trigger the intensity of her sexual drive depending upon the day in her cycle. Her body responds differently, she may have different needs, and she may experience an array of moods. Men need to understand that they, too, have a female side to their emotional being that must be acknowledged and respected. Yet, when you are controlled by pornography, it appears that you and she should always be "on" and ready to perform. In pornography, every time is a great time and every day is a great day. In your rational mind you know that this is unreal, but your thinking is clouded by the addiction. These are unrealistic expectations delivered by a source that is tainted and unnatural.

Do not go to the wasteland of pornography and expect to find information that is helpful emotionally, physically, intellectually, and spiritually. It simply is not there. Just as you would not drink a glass of filthy water, don't partake from the cesspool of pornographic material. And don't proclaim that this filth is healthy or good for you. Drink pure water from the pure source. Get your information from that which is righteous and good.

Points to Consider
1. Do you think pornography is educational?
2. If so, how and why do you believe that it is clean, clear, and healthy information?

3. From where, what, and whom are you getting healthy information regarding sex—information that you know is the truth and not a lie?

51. Scripture Reading: 1 Timothy 4:7-8

PERFORMANCE ANXIETY

Performance anxiety occurs as a result of being too afraid of ourselves. Men who experience this feel inadequate in the bedroom, with intimacy. They may believe they don't perform well as a lover. But it's more than just the performance. They feel insecure about other things, perhaps their personality or the fact that they are unable to share deep feelings. Most often a man who suffers from performance anxiety is unable to connect with his wife at a level that she needs. Perhaps it's because he won't or it's too difficult to talk…or maybe because of the guilt spawned by the addiction to pornography.

Performance anxiety is a very deep-rooted problem that can start with insecurity, lead to a sense of self-worthlessness and, therefore, does affect a man's ability to perform well with his wife on emotional, intellectual, and physical levels. Sometimes impotence is directly related to performance anxiety.

Therefore, to break the lie, a man should ask himself: Why do I need to perform? Why do I need to prove to her what I am? Am I being real or am I living a lie? Have I projected to her (or to others) that I am something other than who I really am? Am I living two separate lives?

Over time, performance anxiety becomes increasingly worse. The insecurity feeds on itself, as does the addiction. The way you go about breaking that is to ask yourself some tough questions: What is real? Who am I? As you engage in self-examination, remember that you are made in the image of God and you do not need to prove who you are through sexual means. You need to enjoy your spouse in natural and intimate ways. Again, do not measure your abilities by what you have seen in pornographic materials—that's not real; it's staged as entertainment.

It's ironic that in pornography, performance anxiety is all fake. There is no real anxiety because the actors are able to do as many "takes" as the director wants; they are able to fine tune the video images as much as they want, making everyone appear beautiful and ever ready to perform. They make everything look so effortless. Yet the lie is the lie. These are not real people. The cameras, makeup, and the digitally enhanced images—all the tricks of Hollywood are used so that performance is beyond what is natural and what the average person experiences. No one fails in pornography, do they? No one loses his or her ability to be outstanding every time. Get rid of these fantasies!

Start appreciating and accepting that you are not a robot but a real human who can feel, laugh, and share. At times sex with your spouse will be phenomenal, and at times you may think it isn't. As long as you have a solid relationship outside of the bedroom, then occasional performance issues will not diminish her love and desire for you. Please note that if you are experiencing performance issues more frequently than you prefer, see your medical doctor. There could be an underlying physiologic condition causing the problem.

Points to Consider

1. What does performance anxiety mean to you? How does it manifest itself?
2. Why is it so important that you prove something to yourself or your wife? What are you trying to prove?
3. What can you do that is real, to share, to be honest so that you don't feel you have to be "number one"?

52. Scripture Reading: Philippians 4:6-7

WHO WOUNDED YOU?

Who wounded you? This is an extremely important question. Oftentimes men who are "into" pornography will have a history of abuse. Someone abused them; therefore, they were exposed to adverse behaviors that led them to pornography. Or maybe it became an escape because they feel so inadequate as a man. Perhaps someone said something to you when you were young that made you feel you are not a whole being or that your genitalia is not normal or that your feelings are not normal or that you are not acceptable and do not measure up to be the heroic man or athlete that everyone expected.

Somewhere there is often an old and deep wound. Pornography becomes an escape—a salve for the wound. It allows you to be (even if only for a short while) whatever you want to be with whatever woman you choose. You can fantasize that a women is extremely desirous of you and wants only you. Unfortunately, using pornography as a balm for your wound does not allow the wound to ever heal.

Why do you use pornography to self-medicate? Because it is readily available—it appeared as a pop-up on your Internet browser, a friend had a magazine, the video was for rent in the motel room while you were on a business trip. And it seemed like something that just might make you feel better. It might make you feel complete…or at least it provided a respite from thinking about the wound. For a while you could pretend and not deal with the wound and its effects on your physical, emotional, and spiritual well-being. But no matter how long you have used pornography, the wound is still there. It hasn't disappeared. The wound continues to fester. And it may even be more infected, contagious, and sore because you are adding filth to it. You are caught in a cycle from which you need to escape.

Wounded hearts are easy hearts to infect. Wounded souls are easy souls to catch.

Points to Consider:

1. What are your wounds? What is the source of these wounds?
2. How do these wounds continue to be open sores through your use of pornography?
3. What would it take for those wounds to be healed, to be forgotten, and even to be transformed into a strength rather than a weakness?

53. Scripture Reading: Psalm 31:9-10

THE STRONGHOLD

The stronghold is the theological term for that which holds us and has the strongest bearing on us. It can be used to refer to demonic forces or to what is leading or gripping us.

With pornography, it is what is holding you, luring you to the addiction. In simple terms, the stronghold is pure lust. Your gratification, your desires, your pleasure through whatever form is all that is important. These comprise the driving force of your addiction and keep you coming back to the computer, the TV, or the magazines.

The stronghold of lust is sin, a sin that has become entangled in your life like blackberry vines around a fence. You can no longer see the fence, and the vines grow every day. When you are encumbered by this stronghold, you are no longer able to engage in rational thought. "I could be doing something else, but I'd rather be on the Internet. I could be doing something more healthy and productive, but I choose to indulge in pornography."

The stronghold overrides; it is dominant; it blocks; it stops that which is good so that it can be perpetuated. In spite of common sense or embarrassment or any risks that you might get caught. The stronghold grips your heart and mind, saying, "I'm first; I want my share; I want my way."

Points to Consider:

1. How strong is the stronghold on you?
2. What does the stronghold look like? Can you describe it?

3. How long has that stronghold been controlling you?
    What parts of your life are controlled? What has it taken
    away from your healthy life so it can be fed?

54. Scripture Reading: Jeremiah 51:53

WHERE DOES IT STOP?

One concern regarding pornography—in fact, this applies to all addictions—is that it is progressive. So what tantalized you at age sixteen or twenty-one or forty-five, whenever you started, no longer arouses you. But the nature of the human body as well as addictions is that you want to achieve the level of pleasure that is necessary. Therefore, like alcohol or any other addiction, it takes more to get the same effect.

Maybe you started out just looking at simple pictures depicting heterosexual encounters, but now the images need to be more graphic. Perhaps now your level of addiction has taken you to looking at pictures or Web sites with children or animals or even orgies and debauchery. Where does it stop? The quick answer is that it doesn't. In my practice I have counseled men who have crossed many lines, not just in their own sense of right and wrong, but have broken the law to feed the addiction that requires more and more of itself. The viewer goes deeper into depravity and guilt, deeper into being consumed by the evil that pornography is and what it represents.

A point comes where a man realizes how far he has gone into the addiction. Yet, because the addiction is so disgusting or so lewd, the secret has to become even greater. The consequences of being discovered are increased. "What would my wife or family or coworkers think if they knew?" Or if you have crossed the line into doing something illegal, you may be asking yourself these questions: "What will happen to me now that I have broken the law? Will I go to jail? Will I be a convicted felon, thereby losing some of my rights as a citizen? Will I lose my family?"

Unfortunately, when you are deep into the addiction, no consequence seems great enough to overcome the power of the addiction. The lure just takes you deeper. It's like a knife going straight to the soul, straight to the very essence of who a man is. The caution here is that this leads to not just spiritual death, but emotional death. And in some extreme cases, physical death as well. The addiction must be stopped before it reaches this point.

Points to Consider

1. How far have you gone in your addiction to pornography—be honest?
2. What does it now take to arouse you when viewing pornography?
3. What is it going to take to stop the addiction?

55. Scripture Reading: Romans 1:28-32

CHAPTER 4

OVERCOMING THE ADDICTION

Larry is a free man now. He's not burdened by a secret that he kept from his wife Claire for twenty years. He no longer has to lie about where he spends his time or money. Most important, he no longer lies to himself about his "need" for pornography. Two years ago Larry came to my office on the brink of losing his family and his job. His secret pastime had been discovered when his company conducted an audit of employees' on-line site visits. When his boss learned that Larry was spending up to four hours a day logged on to pornographic Web sites, Larry could have been fired. Instead, his boss gave Larry another chance. Access blocks were installed on his computer, and Larry was required to participate in counseling.

Though difficult, Larry confessed to Claire about his addiction. For a period of time, the revelation drove a wedge between the two of them. Claire is working to forgive Larry and rebuild their relationship. Through his involvement in an accountability group and our weekly therapy sessions, Larry has learned how to guard his heart and mind from his addiction to pornography. The personal and professional arenas of his life are heading in positive directions, and Larry is the happiest he's been in decades.

FIRST STEP

The first step is to get real—be honest. You have a problem, and that problem is controlling you. That problem is hurting you and your family. The first step is to be truthful with yourself and admit that this is an addiction.

In AA they make you raise your hand and say, "My name is John, and I'm an alcoholic." Perhaps the same step applies here. Try it. "My name is _____, and I'm addicted to pornography." You may make this statement in a men's group, with a therapist, with your pastor, with your wife, with a good friend, or even by yourself with God as your witness.

The important thing is that you take that first step. It will take courage, but think of how your life will change. I, along with many others, will be praying for you.

Points to Consider

1. Am I willing to take this first step?
2. What are the benefits of stepping out?
3. With whom am I going to speak and confide in first?

56. Scripture Reading: Acts 3:19

RISKS OF THE FIRST
STEP OR FUTURE STEPS

There is a risk of revealing your addiction to pornography. You risk rejection or that someone may hold this information over your head. You may risk losing the very thing to which you are addicted. But all of that is a gain in the long run. The risk of continuing your addiction is far worse than any risk of stepping out.

Be very careful in selecting the person to whom you reveal your addiction. Choose the appropriate place and time. Perhaps you want to write out your thoughts beforehand. Find someone with whom you feel safe to confide your secret. Find someone who will love you despite your sin—remember, everyone has sin in his or her life.

Taking that first step is well worth the risk of living a lie that can destroy you and others.

Points to Consider
1. What are the risks? What am I afraid of?
2. How can I overcome the fear of those risks and become courageous?
3. How are you using potential risk as an excuse to remain in your addiction?

57. Scripture Reading: James 1:5; James 4:17

THE D-A-D

Desensitization. After a period of time, pornography makes the individual start to think that the abnormal is now normal. His thinking about sexual activity has become skewed in regard to size of body parts, expectations, positions, or frequency. The person becomes desensitized and immune to the true nature of pornography and the addiction. This then leads to the next phase.

Acceptance. "I think it's OK; I don't mind; it's natural; it's not immoral; it's not wrong; it's all right and I'm fine with my behavior." What was once out of character or not part of the person's normal routine has become acceptable and a regular part of his life. Then comes the subsequent phase.

Distortion. A change occurs in the actual thinking and in the psychological dynamics of the person's brain regarding what he now sees as reality. The irrational has become rational; the illogical has become logical; the unreal becomes real. The person's chemistry is modified.

The same process is true of alcoholism. An alcoholic goes through the same steps: he is desensitized to the need. He says: "I can drink more; it's not going to hurt me. I accept that I drink. It's no big deal. I can afford it, and I want to do it." This use of alcohol and the attitude toward it actually distorts the brain's chemistry. By thinking that he has to have it, he deserves it, he needs it, and he is dependent upon it.

The addictions to pornography and alcohol are very similar because they have the same type of stages in the addiction process. It also should be noted that, unfortunately, one addiction often leads to another.

Points to Consider

1. What stage are you at and how far in are you? Do you have addictive tendencies? Have you ever struggled with another addiction?
2. What have you compromised in your morals and thinking? How far have you strayed from what you truly believe?
3. What are you going to do to get back to what you know is healthy and right so you have clear, godly thinking that is honoring to him?

58. Scripture Reading: Ephesians 4:19

SINCERE REPENTANCE

Repentance is not just saying, "I'm sorry." Repentance is saying that you are going to change your behavior. You confess your sin to yourself, unto the Lord, and to your wife, and you change your behavior. This cannot be accomplished through the flesh. That is done only through the power of the Lord.

Sincere, heartfelt repentance mourns. It cries out. It expresses true sorrow. The Bible tells us that David put ashes on himself or he would lie down in the dirt as a sign of repentance. Is your heart truly willing to lay down your pride and your ego? Is your inner being ready to lie down and say, "I am wrong. I am making choices that are not of the Lord. My actions are not being made from a good and pure heart."

Once you are repentant, God is quick to forgive. Oftentimes wives will forgive and will work to restore the relationship as well. But your behavior must change. Your choices must be different. All of this must come from a repentant heart and asking God to truly help you.

Points to Consider
1. Am I truly repentant?
2. What does that feel and look like?
3. Do I believe that I am forgiven and that I can now move forward with a clean slate?

59. Scripture Reading: 2 Corinthians 7:9; Romans 3:23

THE NATURE OF ADDICTIONS

B e careful when you begin to attack the addiction to pornography that another addiction does not manifest itself. "Since I can no longer have my escape into the Internet or the videos or the chat rooms, I need to fill myself with something else." Sometimes the person starts drinking or taking drugs to escape. Or he may increase the number of cigarettes he smokes. Perhaps his shopping gets out of hand and he is making numerous, impulsive purchases.

Addictive personalities always have a tendency to find a substitute addiction. If it isn't pornography, then it's something else. "I need the rush, the energy, the stress, the guilt from another source." Then the new addiction will begin to feed itself and create its own identity. Even though you are overcoming one addiction, another one is ready to take hold of your life if you are not cautious. So beware when you are working with your therapist or your group that you are addressing your addiction at its root cause, not just the top layers.

Points to Consider

1. Am I increasing my usage of other things, and is this leading to addictive behavior?
2. Do I have an addictive personality (and am not aware of it)?
3. Do I already have other addictions?
4. How am I addressing the root of my addiction(s), the actual reasons I am doing it/them? Am I looking at the cause and not just the result?

60. Scripture Reading: Matthew 12:44-45

REAL PEOPLE

As we discuss pornography and the addiction to it in the recovery process, it's often a revelation when men realize that the people on the video or computer screen are real. They do have first and last names, they have moms, they have dads, they have families, they celebrate Christmas, they go the grocery store. They do the same things we do. But because the pornography industry is profit-driven and it pays these people to act, their true identities are stripped away to create the products in which you are viewing them performing lascivious acts.

What you are seeing is your fantasy—what you want to look at and pretend is real. Part of overcoming the addiction is to realize and take responsibility for what you are doing. You are feeding your money and your time to the pornography industry, a business that exploits people. Even the actors you see who are well-endowed physically have been chosen from thousands of people who auditioned for these roles. They are not average persons; they were selected simply because they are above the norm. Therefore, you should not compare your own or your wife's physical features with those in the pictures. Don't assume that "everyone else" moans while they are engaged in sex or that every encounter is like an Olympic event. Remember, they are actors being paid to do those things. And the photos or screen images have most likely been digitally enhanced—further removing the scenarios you are viewing from real life.

But these also are people created and loved by God, people for whom Jesus died. He cares about them as much as he cares about you. You are responsible for exploiting not only them but yourself as well. I encourage you to make a decision today to stop wasting your time and money, stop exploiting your fellow creations of God, and stop compromising your spirituality. Come back to the real world and learn to appreciate—and respect—all of God's handiwork…including yourself.

Points to Consider

1. Have you ever thought about the people you watch in pornography and who they really might be?
2. Have you become numb to your own conscience so that you don't see them as being real people?
3. Do you realize that you are exploiting yourself and them by participating in this addiction?

61. Scripture Reading: Matthew 7:12; Luke 6:31

SPIRITUAL INVENTORY

This is an exercise wherein you evaluate yourself and your life. Such inventories ask you to write about where you are and where you want to be in your career, in your relationships, in your finances, in your physical being, in your social life, and in your spiritual life.

There are various self-assessment inventories that you can complete (usually working with your therapist or your employer's Human Resources department) to help guide you through the process of examining your personal, professional, and spiritual life. This is literally taking a pad of paper and writing about your life. "This is who I am." Questions may include: What does my life look like? How do I spend my time? Where do I spend my energy? What are my priorities? What is important? What is not important? How do I resolve conflict? What do I like? What do I dislike? What do I want to accomplish in the future? What are my goals? How is my addiction to pornography not supporting my goals?

An inventory is a thinking-and-writing exercise that may take months to complete. It is a process that requires you to think things through and then reread and reflect on the content. Over the course of time, you will likely add and subtract in order to capture what you want to say about yourself. It's not something you do quickly, but the insight you gain is worth the time and effort.

154 · CONQUERING PORNOGRAPHY:
OVERCOMING THE ADDICTION

Points to Consider

1. When am I going to start my inventory?
2. What would be on my list of topics I want to cover?
3. Start writing on each of those topics.

62. Scripture Reading: Matthew 12:36

TELL YOUR SECRET TO SOMEONE

I n Alcoholics Anonymous there is a saying: "You are only as sick as your first and deepest secret." This is a true statement. Addiction to pornography is a huge secret. You keep it from your family, your church congregation, your coworkers, everyone. You are not proud of the addiction. You hide the material. You have created computer passwords so others cannot know the sites you visit. It's a secret that is often kept for years. It's time to tell your secret to someone now!

As human beings, especially men, we know that when we verbalize something, it is brought into the open. When sin is brought out of the darkness, it loses its power. It also helps you gain freedom. Confiding in another man, your wife, your pastor, or a therapist—someone you trust— allows you to be honest about your addiction.

"I have a problem and I'm scared. I am now going to be real. I know that if I don't address this problem, it is going to destroy me." The secret may take years to destroy you. But the longer you wait to reveal the secret, the more momentum and strength it gains. The more you hold on to it, the further the addiction becomes engrained in all aspects of your life.

Telling someone is risky. What if the person betrays you and shares your secret? What if you learn that the person cannot be trusted? That is a genuine risk. But I believe that telling your secret to someone is worth the risk. Your only other option is to keep the secret, and that will only lead to self-destruction. Use discretion and try to find the most trustworthy person to whom you can tell your secret. Perhaps the person should be a professional who is bound by confidentiality laws to protect your secret. Nevertheless, you must move forward and tell your secret to someone. Please do it as soon as possible!

Points to Consider
1. How deep is your secret?
2. To whom are you going to tell your secret? When?
3. Are you going to be fully honest, or tell only half of the truth?

63. Scripture Reading: James 5:16

THE TRIGGERS THAT KEEP YOU HOOKED

Triggers are sneaky. They are not always as obvious as they may sound. They are the many things that cause you to go to your addiction for release. It may be stress or loneliness or the inability to express yourself sexually in appropriate ways or conflict in a relationship or work-related issues that bring you down. Perhaps you think you deserve your use of pornography because it is a reward for hard work you have done.

What are the triggers that cause you to be drawn toward pornography? For some it is habit—it's simply become a lifestyle. You may even be unaware of how the pattern of use became so ingrained in your everyday life. It may be fulfilling fantasies, such as finding yourself alone in a hotel room with time and opportunity to engage in pornography. Or perhaps you have found that a neighbor has high-speed Internet service and your computer can link up to the Internet via "free" wireless access to pornographic sites. You believe you will not be caught in any of these practices. How convenient!

What are the triggers that feed your addiction? Recognizing *and* stopping those triggers is key to becoming healthy. Having the ability to say, "I know this is something that leads me to using pornography. What can I put in its place?"

If your trigger is stress, could you replace pornography with exercise and go to the gym? If it is anxiety, with whom can you talk about the causes of your anxiety rather than using pornography as a fake release? Your options are endless. Perhaps this is a good point to seek professional advice to help identify the causes and triggers that make you stumble, and learn how to overcome them in healthy ways.

Points to Consider

1. What are your triggers? List them on a piece of paper.
2. How often do you find yourself stumbling due to those triggers and using pornography as a false release?
3. What healthy choice can you substitute for each of the triggers to your addiction?
4. Could you call an accountability buddy when you are tempted by a trigger? Have you identified a buddy?

*64. Scripture Reading: 1 Corinthians 6:18;
Matthew 5:28-29*

DON'T TALK, TAKE ACTION

M any of us have talked and talked and talked about something we are going to do. Perhaps it is to lose weight. Or we are going to save money. Or we are going to work toward earning a higher education or a promotion. Or we talk about taking our wife on a date. Or we are going to be more sensitive.

Guys, cut the talk. Take action. There comes a point in your addiction to pornography when you have to say, "I'm tired of saying the prayers—'Lord, please forgive me'—or of admitting to my wife that I have a problem and promising to stop." Talk is cheap. Action requires action. That means there is a risk. That means you have to get off your backside. You have to do something tangible. You have to make it happen. You have to join the group. You must make an appointment with that therapist. You need to create an accountability relationship with that brother in Christ. You have to throw the garbage out of the house. You have to clean up your computer and put some filters on it. You have to make a plan. You have to take action. You must do something real that has definite steps she can see.

Repeatedly saying you are sorry for the last year or sixteen years really isn't taking action. What are you going to do? How are you going to stick to your plan?

The other thing about taking action is that you have to be consistent. Whatever you choose to do must be done on a regular basis, and you have to do it long term. If you want to work out and get stronger abs, it doesn't happen in twenty minutes once a year when you are in the mood.

It happens through a plan. Create a definite plan that is realistic and has expectations. And then stick to it.

I promise that you will succeed. It's hard work. Sometimes you are going to resist keeping with your plan. Most likely you are going to say, "Well, I have reasons." No. Once you make a commitment to overcome this addiction, you must persevere. The results are worth it. You will be in a much deeper relationship with your wife, guilt and bondage free. I encourage you to take action today.

Points to Consider

1. How long have I been talking and not taking action?
2. What action am I willing to take? Do I need someone to help me take my first steps?
3. Am I really going to stick with my plan? What commitment am I going to make?
4. What will the cost be if I don't take action and just keep talking? What will the results of that be?
5. What results do I want to see in six months, in a year, in a lifetime? Set those goals.

65. Scripture Reading: James 2:26

CAN I CHANGE?

C an I change? *Yes!* There is always hope. God wants you to have peace and joy. He wants you to live without anxiety and guilt. But based on my years of counseling, I have to tell you that you cannot change without God. Oh, you can "white knuckle" it for a while. But real change comes from the heart. That requires God's help and strength.

You've tried so hard to keep your secret. Isolation has become a habit, and this has separated you from quality relationships with your wife, family, and God. You cannot change by yourself—the isolation has to stop. The issues need to be revealed and dealt with in the open. That does not mean public disgrace. You need support and love, not judgment.

Fear has held you captive from admitting the addiction, from getting help, from changing. You may be afraid of rejection or your reputation or that she will leave you. Whatever the fear is, face it straight on. Start with a trusted friend or leader in your church. Seek a therapist to counsel with—the law protects your confidentiality and privacy. Do not be afraid to get help. Move beyond the shame and guilt. Don't let anything or anyone hold you back.

Many men have come in my office and asked for reassurance that their secret is safe. What do I do with the notes? Is there any way this can come back and haunt them? I give them all the reassurance I can. Some of my patients choose to use an alias name and pay for their treatment in cash. Their fears are real, and they have a right to be protected. The primary objective is to get on with the process of healing and being restored. Your wife, family, and friends want you to succeed. Be of good courage…you can change. Make the choice today!

Points to Consider

1. What are your fears?
2. How much do you want help? Are you ready?
3. From what sources are you going to seek help?

66. Scripture Reading: Philippians 4:13

CLEANING THE HOUSE

C leaning the house is a process where you gather all the videotapes, paraphernalia, and magazines—everything you have that supports your habit—and literally destroy it.

Here at the office I have people, for accountability reasons, bring these items into the office to take a strong step toward the authenticity of overcoming the addiction. I have had some men bring in *National Geographic* magazines, thinking that I wouldn't look in the box, or video covers that were empty. I have learned all the tricks people use to deny or hold on to the addiction. After the man leaves my office, I destroy the material by disposing of it in a dumpster that is not accessible to the public.

The bottom line is that you have to get that stuff physically out of the house. You have to clean the C drive on the computer and have filters and codes to prohibit you from accessing or loading the material again. You have to not hide that stuff in the garage or wherever. Only then can you get it out of your mind and heart—and out of your life for good!

You can't just move it to another spot or ask someone to hide it from you. Remember that this is an addiction. If you don't remove the pornographic materials, they will continue to have a stronghold on you; you will continue to be tempted; and it will remain a part of your life. So take that first step: Clean the house!

Points to Consider

1. What are you trying to hide, and why is it hidden someplace secretive?
2. When are you going to get rid of it?
3. Who are you going to give it to so that you have some accountability? Will this person know whether or not you got rid of it all?
4. Do you have a plan to avoid temptation?

67. *Scripture Reading: Hebrews 10:22; 2 Timothy 2:21*

THE GRIEVING PROCESS

You probably already know that at some point pornography became a friend. For most people addicted to pornography, it becomes something you rely on for entertainment, for comfort, for escape, for reducing stress. It almost mirrors a real friend. But it's not. It's a substitute that you play a game with—much like an alcoholic will call the bottle his friend. In the process of overcoming your addiction, you have to say good-bye to that friend. And that involves a grieving process.

We all grieve the loss of something that was once dear to us. Most often this is a person. It could be a job or a home. We grieve many things and at many levels. Grieving the loss of a sin, the loss of an addiction (friend) requires basically the same four stages as any grief.

First, there is denial. Well, you have passed that already by reading this book and admitting you have a problem with pornography.

The second step is anger. That's a very large step because you have to fight with yourself and with the pornography. You blame yourself for getting caught up in it. Or you blame God for not rescuing you sooner. Maybe you blame your wife or your girlfriend because she didn't meet your needs the way you wanted—in a real or fantasy way. You blame society for making it so easy for you to fall down and get caught and for creating a stumbling block. Your anger will take many, many forms.

The third stage you move on to is acceptance. Acceptance is saying, "I acknowledge this problem; I can grieve over it; and I accept a new way of building my life."

The fourth stage is rebuilding. You might ask yourself, "Where am I going to go from here?" As you have already seen in this book, the key theme is to build healthy relationships that can take the place of the artificial.

No one has the opportunity to grieve by going through these steps sequentially: one, two, three, four. You'll grieve in steps one, two, three, two, four, one, two, two. You'll bounce around, maybe to several steps on any given day. But you want to move on from the anger into the acceptance and rebuilding. This takes time. You need to express that anger; you need to have people validate it; and you need to understand that it's real.

How we handle our anger is the key. There is destructive and constructive behavior. Obviously, constructive behavior is acceptable; destructive behavior is not acceptable. So any time you are hurting yourself, someone else, or a thing, it is destructive. This needs to be refocused into another area, which will be addressed in other chapters of this book.

Believe in yourself: You can overcome this addiction.

Points to Consider

1. Have you admitted that pornography was a friend? In what ways was it your friend?
2. What stage of the grieving process are you in now?
3. How can you move on to acceptance and rebuilding your life?
4. What are you doing to make real friends?

68. Scripture Reading: 2 Corinthians 12:21

TEMPTATION TO ACT OUT

Many statistical analyses and materials state that men who act out sexually—pedophiles, rapists, prostitutes—have gotten ideas or been stimulated by pornography. Other men would say that they would never go that far and would never cross that line.

Yet each of us is weak. Each person has a vulnerable side, a day, a moment in which he falls prey to temptation. Perhaps you were away on a business trip or you had a friendship that slipped into a physical attraction or relationship. The temptation for acting out affects all men—no one is immune to this type of acting out. We operate on impulses. Sometimes our actions are well thought out and planned, but sometimes it strikes us when we least expect it, and we are the ones who are surprised.

Pornography gives a basis for acting out in the real world in the flesh. The risks of acting out are even greater and more treacherous than anything we can ever imagine.

Points to Consider

1. What are my risks of acting out?
2. Am I honest in admitting that this could happen to me even by surprise?
3. What safeguards do I have in place so that I won't act out, knowing that I will regret it?

69. Scripture Reading: Mark 14:38

WHEN IT IS TOO LATE

A man had a tragic, fatal accident at work. He had never prepared for the possibility of this happening. As his wife and family went through the garage, they found his pornography. His grandchildren were the ones who stumbled across the secret stash months after his passing. They were shocked and disappointed. Their discovery profoundly affected the memory they kept of this man.

If something similar happened to you, what would your family find in the closet or the garage or the computer? What would be your legacy? Would you be embarrassed if your mother found pornography in your dresser drawers when she was cleaning out your apartment? Would you feel humiliated if someone got on your computer and found materials hidden in secret, password-protected folders?

You probably think there will always be time and opportunity to get rid of the evidence or the addiction before something bad happens. But what if you are wrong? It's a sobering thought. I pray that it is a life-altering revelation. With all sincerity, I can tell you that your family will be heartbroken if they discover pornography among your things. Is this how you want to be remembered?

You would never intentionally do something to hurt or embarrass your family, would you? So why hang on to pornographic materials that will undermine their respect for you and rob them of loving memories? Clean the house. Clean your heart. Clean your mind. You have the power to change your destiny and the legacy you leave behind.

Points to Consider

1. Have I fooled myself into thinking I will have time to get rid of the pornographic materials I have hidden?
2. What can I do today to protect my family from discovering my materials?
3. How do I want to be remembered?

70. Scripture Reading: 1 Corinthians 5:7

LAW OF DIMINISHING RETURNS

The more you are into pornography, the more you need. Like any other addiction, what was attractive in the beginning is no longer stimulating. It doesn't get your juices flowing, so you need more and more. That's the nature of all addictions, but in pornography it takes more stimuli, more graphic materials. It starts to cross serious lines into the grotesque and absurd. Eventually it becomes so disgusting that even the person addicted to pornography realizes that the materials are beyond belief.

With the Internet and other technologies, everything is available. The wildest, ugliest, dirtiest, filthiest fantasy can be sought out—and found. The law of diminishing returns dictates that you can never go back to the simple, innocent days or the things that once attracted you. You only continue to want more. More time, more things, more of whatever.

Once hooked into the spiral of diminishing returns, you cannot gradually get out. You can't just say, "I'm going to cut back." No one cuts back gradually. That is a lie. To overcome, you must stop completely, cold turkey...*now!*

Points to Consider
1. What are the diminishing returns in your addiction?
2. How has the addiction progressed in your life to become more graphic and more disgusting?
3. How are you going to stop the diminishing returns and get away from the addiction?

71. Scripture Reading: Romans 1:28-32

DEAL WITH THE ANGER

Anger is a very deep emotion. For many men, it is one of the only three they express: happiness, anger, or love. Anger is an acceptable emotion to have, but it is how we deal with the anger that is most significant.

Coming to grips with your addiction to pornography is going to create anger. You may be angry at a variety of things. It's a step in the grieving process as you let go of the addiction that has become so much a part of your life. The four steps of grief are the following: 1) Denial, which you have already passed because you are addressing your anger; 2) Anger; 3) Accepting and negotiating; 4) What am I going to do about my situation, and how am I going to rebuild? Grieving is a process, because you are literally leaving an old friend. Despite the fact that your "friend" is evil and destructive, it's a friend you have known well and made a significant part of your life. It's a friend that provided you temporary pleasure at a heavy, heavy price.

The anger you feel is genuine and may be directed at the pornography industry, at the person who got you started in your addiction, perhaps at the person who abused you (if applicable), at your wife or past failed relationships, at the fact that you were caught and now must be accountable. The anger can go many directions, but you absolutely must deal with it. You must not ignore the anger or try to shove it down. If you do not deal with your anger, it could manifest itself as depression. In addition, misguided anger could be transferred to other people unjustly.

Your anger is real. What you do with it is a choice. You can talk about it, you can share it, you can cry, you can engage in a variety of physical activities for release, but most of all, the anger must be recognized for what it is and it must be processed. If it is not, the anger will consume you and defeat you.

Some men who have not dealt appropriately with their anger have become so frustrated that they return to the addiction, hoping to appease the anger. Instead, they compound the anger and they have gone deeper into addiction.

Points to Consider

1. Are you angry? What is the source of that anger?
2. How are you expressing your anger? Are you using constructive or destructive methods?
3. What is it going to take for you to resolve your anger over time? Do you have a process in place?

72. Scripture Reading: Ephesians 4:26-27

DRIVE BY THE TEMPTATION

D o not think you can justify partial recovery. It is truly all or none. An alcoholic does not work in a liquor store. An alcoholic does not go into a bar and think he or she is going to order just a cola. It's the same for someone addicted to pornography. You must drive by the temptation.

If your regular route home takes you by a store that sells pornography, change the way you drive to and from your house. If there is a bookstore or magazine stand you have frequented, find another path for your daily walk. Clear the computer and add accountability filters. Put safeguards in place that address all your triggers so you are able to "drive by the temptation" no matter where it is. You will know that if you go to that store or visit that Web site, certain things will happen. You will be able to say to yourself, "If I go there, then this and this will happen; therefore, I am accountable."

Driving by the temptation is a discipline to which you will grow accustomed over time. It is likely that the first few times you will try to justify and rationalize. "This doesn't affect me. I don't have to do this. I'm above this." You are lying to yourself. The only way to have victory over temptation and over the addiction is to change your patterns of behavior. You must start anew.

If you do stumble, which many people do, you just start over. Do not give up hope. "I fell down; I fell in the hole. The next time I took a different road to avoid the hole."

Points to Consider

1. What are my patterns?
2. What are the physical locations and/or computer sites that I visit and how can I "drive" by them?
3. What can I put in place to make me accountable to myself and others so that if I don't drive by or if I stop there will be a consequence?

73. Scripture Reading: 1 Corinthians 6:18-20

WHY DO I FEEL SHAME?

Among the basic emotions that most people feel are embarrassment, being ashamed, and shame. Embarrassment occurs when someone is caught picking his nose or passing gas in public. A person may become flustered and say things like, "Oh, man, that's gross. Sorry." We just let it go because even though we feel embarrassed, it's not really a big deal and people usually just overlook the faux pas with understanding and a little chuckle.

Feeling ashamed goes a bit deeper. "I'm ashamed that I got caught by the IRS," or "I lied to a friend, and he called me on it." Or perhaps, "I'm ashamed that I blew up at a coworker, and now I must go back and apologize." Feeling ashamed is usually followed by a healthy dose of guilt—or the person pays a fine or goes to prison or apologizes. The individual is redeemed once the consequence is paid.

Shame is much deeper. It is a feeling that "I am the broken Christmas toy that no one wants. I'm defective. There is something wrong with me."

The addiction to pornography creates all three emotions. "Oh, I'm a little embarrassed because someone saw me or I slipped and made an inappropriate joke." "I'm ashamed that I have become involved in pornography." "I'm ashamed that I was caught." But deeper down, you are dealing with feelings of inadequacy. "I'm shamed. I feel inadequate as I look at the pictures or when I'm on the phone engaged in telephone sex or when I'm on line in the sex chat rooms." There is a sense of insecurity that feeds your shame. That shame erodes your self-esteem and strength. It erodes the confidence you need to overcome the addiction.

Part of being victorious is to ask yourself: "What am I ashamed of? Where did that seed come from? How can I overcome it?" You need to remind yourself of the positive things by saying, "I am a child of God. I do have hope. I don't need this addiction and filth in my life. I am not broken. I am merely a man who needs to grow in areas where I have never grown before."

Points to Consider

1. What does your shame feel like?
2. Do you feel like the broken toy? When did that start? Who made you feel like that?
3. How do I overcome the shame and believe that I am complete in God?

74. Scripture Reading: Psalm 40:12

SIN IS NOT THE ISSUE

I hear this all the time from men: "It's not sin. It's just something I do. Well, maybe it's an issue, but I don't think it's really anything wrong to do. It's certainly not sin."

Men, let me tell you that it *is* a sin. It's the sin of lust; it's the sin of adultery in your heart and mind; it's the sin of fornication, of stepping outside your relationship. It is a sin and one that needs to be repented of and brought out into the open.

In today's culture there is the tendency to minimize or sanitize our issues because we don't want to face them. In fact, we often call them something else, hoping that whatever it is will be considered something less than a sin. Yet when you examine pornography for what it really is—it is destructive and it is a sin. The Bible says that the wages of sin is death—not always physical death, but death of your spirit, death of your relationship, death of your heart. The sin exacts a huge price, and it costs you dearly.

Therefore, don't hide behind another euphemism. Let's see it for what it is and call it what it is—a sin that is sure to separate you from your wife, your family, and the Lord.

Points to Consider
1. Do you consider the use of pornography a sin?
2. In what terms is it a sin?
3. Is engaging in pornography adultery and fornication? Do you understand that it breaks the bonds of your marriage?

75. Scripture Reading: 1 John 2:16

WALK ON THE BEACH

I love the ocean and always have. A walk on the beach is a time of reflection. It's a time when a person can review his goals, recharge his battery, and restore his soul. It's a time of gaining strength.

A significant initial step in overcoming any addiction or problem is to clear your head. Get some fresh air. Exercise your muscles. In my opinion, there is no better place to do this than at the beach. Some people would prefer to walk in the woods or go bicycle riding. It doesn't matter what you do or where you go. But you need to do something that helps you become healthier mentally, spiritually, and physically.

Take some time for reflecting, reevaluating the decisions you are making, reviewing the past and learning from it, and looking to the future. In my work with people, I know that taking time out for this is not done often enough. Each of us needs this time in our lives to grow and to heal. This step in overcoming your addiction is just as essential as throwing out the pornographic materials or erasing the computer files.

Your journey to a healthy future begins with the first step, so take a walk today.

Points to Consider

1. Where could I walk that would be most effective for me?
2. What would I want to accomplish?
3. How do I recharge my emotional and spiritual battery?

76. Scripture Reading: Matthew 14:23

WHEN THE COMPUTER SCREAMS AT YOU

One of the things that you must consider regarding an addiction—whether it be to pornography or the gambling tables or to any other vice—is that the person with the addiction has the sense that his favorite source of feeding the addiction is "screaming" at him to engage in the activity. The addiction screams from the shelves if it is a bottle of alcohol or from the casino as you drive by on your way home from work.

The computer may be singing its "siren song" to you tonight: "Come over and check your e-mail. There may be an important message you don't want to miss. Just spend a few minutes. Don't you have to do some work on that presentation for tomorrow's meeting?" What you are really doing is rationalizing your craving to hit a few of your favorite sites real quick before someone sees that you are on the computer.

A crucial step in becoming victorious over the addiction is to avoid turning on the computer when it is screaming at you. Do not even attempt to fool yourself or anyone else by saying you are going to check e-mail or work on a project. You and I both know that your favorite sites are just one or two clicks away. Stay away from the computer if it is your gateway to addiction. Someone who is a recovering alcoholic cannot work in a liquor store or as a bartender.

During those times when the computer is screaming at you to feed your addiction, find another activity. Talk with someone about what you are experiencing. Work through the fact that the computer is "begging" you to come to it.

This is a physical, emotional, and spiritual battle that you can win on your way to freedom.

Points to Consider

1. When does the computer most often scream at you, tempting you to visit your favorite sites?
2. Do you recognize that the computer is just a lure, waiting for you to bite and be taken for bait?
3. What is your plan when the computer screams at you? What activity will you engage in instead of responding to the lure of pornography?

77. Scripture Reading: Ephesians 5:3-12

WHITE KNUCKLING IT

White knuckling is a concept that comes from Alcoholics Anonymous that says, "I can prove to myself and to the world and to her that I am OK." It's literally just holding on. You may say things like: "See? I've been without it now for two weeks. See? I don't need it; I've been without it for five weeks." You are holding on just to prove to someone that you are not addicted. This is a lie.

The practice of white knuckling does not deal with the actual issues. You are not dealing with the facts or the causes of your addiction. It's just hanging on, a way of holding your breath so you can say, "I'm not addicted; I'm OK." White knuckling is a lie. You must find the courage to say, "I need to let go. I need to admit my addiction. I need to get some help." In fact, you may have to tell yourself, "I need to fall as far as I need to fall so that I can hit the bottom and be able to seek the help I need to turn my life around. Now I can be honest with myself rather than trying to prove to everyone what I am not."

Honesty is a key word in your recovery. Letting go and letting God is not just a trite phrase in rebuilding your life.

Points to Consider

1. Am I white knuckling it right now?
2. What am I trying to prove and to whom?
3. When am I going to let go and actually deal with the real issues?

78. Scripture Reading: 1 John 1:9; Philippians 4:8-9

FREEDOM MEANS

Emotional, mental, and spiritual freedom from the bondage of a sin such as pornography is sometimes lost in the translation when the man is in the midst of that sin. He forgets what it is like to "fly" without feeling guilt or to be able to walk into a room or to know there are no secrets—to truly have a freedom within himself and a freedom within a relationship that says, "Everything is OK."

I remember a story of a wife who came home and told her husband that her vaginal area was burning. His comment was, "Well, you didn't get it from me." She immediately began to cry. Her husband backed up and realized how what he had said sounded to her. He then said, "Oh, honey, I didn't mean that you got something on your own. I wasn't accusing you. I was just saying that I haven't done anything that I am ashamed of. Please go to the doctor and find out what is wrong, and don't be afraid."

She stopped crying and said to her husband, "The reason I'm crying is because I know that it isn't from you. I trust you and there is a bond between us."

Later that week she went to the doctor and found out that her condition was the result of reaction to soap that was used at they gym she had recently joined. It was nothing to be concerned about.

Both the husband and wife were free—free to be truly honest with each other and free to not be embarrassed in taking the question to the doctor.

In an addiction there is a bondage, a secret, a darkness that hides inside you and eats away at your mind and soul. It strips you of the true freedom you can have in Christ.

Points to Consider

1. What would freedom feel like without the addiction?
2. Write down what you would do if you were totally free.
3. How can I become free from this addiction?

79. Scripture Reading: Galatians 5:1

LEAVE

Putting aside your sin—or the temptation to commit sin—is often a physical choice, not just a mental or spiritual one. I think of the story of Joseph, the young Hebrew man first enslaved but then given charge by the Pharaoh over Egypt. When first taken into Egypt, he served in the house of Potiphar (who was captain of the guard for Pharaoh). Potphar's wife tried to seduce Joseph. He knew that her attraction to him was wrong, so, according to the Bible, Joseph left. In fact, the account says that he fled from her.

Pornography is a seducing, tantalizing type of pleasure. Though it looks wonderful on the surface, men, you must leave it behind. You must choose to flee from it. Literally, you must get up and get away from the computer; you must not pull into the X-rated video store's parking lot; you must stop purchasing pornographic magazines.

You must physically and mentally leave. Once you are out, do not look back. Don't think about what you may be missing. Think about the monster that almost devoured you. If you were to see a wild animal, would you try to wrestle with it? No. You would try to escape as soon as possible. Do not think that pornography is not a roaring lion waiting to kill you and anyone else who falls prey to the addiction. As a godly man, you need to leave.

Points to Consider

1. What is your plan in the event that the temptation to use pornography attacks you?

2. Have you ever left your addiction to pornography? How has that felt?

3. How are you going to leave it now—once and for all?

80. *Scripture Reading: 2 Timothy 2:22; Genesis 19:17*

NOTHING REPLACES IT

There's an interesting twist with pornography because people in the throes of the addiction constantly need to feed themselves with material that is bigger, better, more graphic, and more scintillating in order to achieve the "high" they crave and have come to expect. With cocaine and heroin, the pattern is that the first hit is always the best and most thrilling. One of the reasons drug addicts overdose is that they increase the amount they take or combine it with alcohol or other drugs to duplicate that original high. The same pattern emerges when a young person discovers sex. Oftentimes an adult will remember the thrill of that first experience or the first years of a new marriage and try to recreate the feeling by having affairs. Or as the initial exuberance wanes, a man may try to replace it with pornography.

The bottom line is that nothing will ever provide the same high as the first time of anything. Telling yourself that increasing the usage or intensity or volume will bring you back to the initial feeling is a lie. Trying to achieve this is a huge waste of time and energy. No matter how you try to enhance the experience, the initial high cannot be duplicated. When you work to overcome the addiction, I know you will grieve for that high and believe that nothing will ever replace it. What you have to do is accept that this is part of the loss, part of the grieving, and that part of giving up the addiction is abandoning the search for the high you once found so appealing but now has become a negative factor in your life.

What replaces an addiction is healthy relationships with healthy people and living a healthy life. What replaces it is not having any involvement with pornography. Spend your time on activities that are fulfilling, projects that are rewarding. Find ways of expressing your feelings and not being isolated, ways of dealing with anger or sexual insecurities. Associate with people you love and can talk with and be real with.

People who are involved with pornography live two lives (the chapter "The Secret, The Lie" speaks specifically to this). They hide the addiction and pretend it doesn't exist. What replaces it is genuine relationships that are growing and healthy.

Points to Consider
1. What are you trying to replace your addiction to pornography with?
2. What is not working?
3. What will work if you try to find an appropriate replacement?

81. Scripture Reading: James 1:14-16

APOLOGIZE TO HER

You must be honest with yourself, and you must be honest to her—your wife—about what you have done. She will be deeply hurt because of your involvement with pornography and may become angry because of her pain. You need to apologize for violating your marriage vows. You made a covenant between you and her and with God, and you did this before friends and family. Now, according to Scripture, you have broken that covenant by making the marriage bed unholy in your heart and in your body.

Your apology needs to be genuine, sincere, heartfelt, and real. Many men will try to placate their wives by saying they are sorry only because that is what is expected. But these apologies don't have any substance and no long-term commitment to change. Don't underestimate your wife. Women possess a "sixth sense," so your wife probably already knew that there was something happening with you sexually that had taken you outside of the marriage. She can read you like a book. Yet she may have avoided confronting you due to a fear of rejection, working through her own feelings, or personalizing your behavior by thinking that maybe she just wasn't meeting your needs because she doesn't look or act like the women in the fantasies shown in pornographic materials.

She is hurt. In fact, she feels violated. She has experienced a form of sexual abuse. Even though you may not categorize it as such because you didn't "actually" touch another woman, the reality is that you were intimate with another women with your eyes, with your heart, with your emotions, with your fantasies, and with your sexuality. No matter what you think, if you are sincerely repentant, you need to accept that she feels violated and she has a reason to feel hurt.

It may take a long time for her to accept your apology. Do not expect immediate results—and don't get angry if she doesn't offer instant forgiveness. It could take months or even a year and many discussions, questions, fears, and tears for her to work through the pain of this experience. All of these must occur for her to heal. It is also critical to the healing of your marriage and to your own sexuality and psyche.

To begin the road to your own recovery, you must first apologize to her. When you do, you can start to close the door to the past and open the door to your future.

Points to Consider

1. When you apologized to her, were you totally honest?
2. When you apologized to her, were you more concerned about her feelings than your own?
3. When you apologized, did you genuinely mean that you will stop using pornography, or were you just placating her so you could continue your behavior?
4. When you apologized, was it complete or was it filled with excuses and justification and blaming her? Remember, your addiction was never her fault—you made the choice and you own the responsibility.

82. Scripture Reading: 1 Corinthians 7:2-3; 1 Peter 3:7

DESIRE ONLY HER

The way to completely overcome an addiction is to put something better in its place. To me, this is probably the most essential part of the entire healing process.

That something better is your wife and the love you have for her. Make her the center of your universe—second only to God. Give her the priority she deserves. Rather than expressing your sexuality, feelings, or emotions through pornography, share them with her. Desire only her. Make her the focus of your world and your love.

Renew your commitment to her and to your marriage. Focus your words, your deeds, your kindness, and your sexuality on her…don't just see her as a physical person, but see her as a total person with a mind, with goals, with needs, with a heart, and with feelings. She is more than just a person of the flesh; she is a living child of the Lord. You need to look at her as Christ regards her—beautiful and precious. Treat her as though it is a privilege to know her and to be with her. Put your wife in her rightful place as the center of your universe and the *only* woman you love and desire.

Points to Consider

1. Is your wife your priority, second only to God?
2. How can you love and cherish her more?
3. How can you view her as a complete, total person? What does that mean?

83. Scripture Reading: Proverbs 5:18-19

SPIRITUAL RETREAT

Henry Nouwen is the author of a book entitled *Out of Solitude* that has changed the lives of many people. His main premise is that we need to have a quiet retreat away from the crowds, away from work, even away from family to be alone with the Father, just as Christ spent time with him while he was here on Earth. A spiritual retreat is a time that may be spent at the beach or the mountains, someplace where you can go for a long walk without any interruptions or concerns for time or food preparation or for anything that could distract you.

I have taught many people what has been an effective spiritual-growth time for myself. Gather some basic foods that require no preparation, take your Bible, and tuck away a pen and paper. Then take a long walk and listen to what the Lord has to say to you. Read passages of Scripture that you find very meaningful—ones the Holy Spirit leads you to. Take notes or journal your thoughts. Write some questions. Let the experience unveil itself to you. There is no specific formula, and what one person likes another may not. The first day or even the first few times may feel awkward, but once you understand and get into the pace of having that time alone with God, you will find how healing, rejuvenating, and rich the time is.

Don't take anyone with you; you need to be alone with God. You need to have a concentrated time of just you with the Father. No distractions. No TV. No radio. No movies. Just you and the Lord, because that is when you can best hear him and he can hear you.

I encourage you to take a spiritual retreat as soon as possible. Discover what God wants to say to you. Let him give you the strength to overcome your addiction.

Points to Consider

1. Plan a spiritual retreat. What would it look like for you? Where would you go? How soon can you take the retreat?

2. What would you want to accomplish if you went on a retreat?

3. Are you willing to pray that your heart would be open to what God wants to give you and to receive his help in healing your addiction?

84. Scripture Reading: Daniel 9:3

RECOVERY AND ACCOUNTABILITY GROUPS

Groups to aid in recovery can be a positive and a negative. The advantage of a group is that you have people who are in the same situation and are on the same walk. They can help you identify with your grief. Group members can oftentimes provide insight to each other; they can share ideas; and you are not alone. The disadvantage of groups is that sometimes they spend more time belaboring the sin than they do addressing the solutions.

Be sure that you find a group with a strong leader—one who acts as the head of the group. There is one particular group I knew of in a church. The group was foundering. It became obvious that it was the blind leading the blind. It was the drowning trying to save the drowning. There needs to be a facilitator who perhaps has overcome the addiction to pornography himself or a skilled person who has never had an addiction to pornography but is able to lead an effective group. Pick your group carefully.

Groups are available through churches, Focus on the Family, Promise Keepers; many therapists will have groups through their clinics. You just have to do some research and find out what is in your area. But be sure the group is biblically based and that they have a focus and a purpose. The ultimate goal is to hold each other accountable and to have success in not falling back into addiction. You do not want to be involved in a group where men just get together to whine and complain or just to have a social evening.

Groups have positives and negatives. You want to evaluate each group carefully before becoming involved. Some of the key things in a group that are difficult for me are that the participants often speak in code and don't really open up to others. They talk in the third person, or they don't say exactly what they want to say. They beat around the bush. So you want to find a group that is going to deal with the issues straight on and is composed of people who are going to be honest. Another challenge is that honesty takes time. You have to learn to trust your group, and that takes time. Therefore, men oftentimes won't go to a group or they won't follow through. They'll say it didn't work out. "I tried it three times and I don't want to go anymore." You have to stick with it and put effort into making the group work for you. Try to make eye contact with other members; try to be direct; try to be sincere.

I don't want to discourage you with the following sad story; I think it will make a strong point. A man named "Doug" was afraid of having his addiction exposed. His wife prodded him to join a group. He went to the meeting and did open up and begin to talk. Another participant, "Mike," shared what he heard with his wife. Soon many people throughout the church knew about Doug's problem. Confidentiality was breeched. Doug was hurt and angry; he felt judged. Consequently, he left the church. Make sure your group has rules. The rules must include confidentiality, trust, opening up, not judging. There must be a commitment to the efforts of each member to overcome the addiction to be victorious for the long term.

Some groups will last for years because they grow deeper and deeper. They may work through a variety of books such as this one. Make sure your group is going to work, and don't be afraid to put some things in place to make it a trustful environment and worthwhile experience.

Points to Consider

1. What kind of group are you specifically looking for? What qualities would meet your needs?
2. What groups in your area match your criteria for meeting times and focus? Do the research.
3. Evaluate the leader. Is the leader godly? Is he focused? Does he know what he is talking about? Does he address the heart of the issues, or is he merely superficial?
4. Does the group have a written set of benchmarks or goals, timeframes, things they can look at and know they are making progress? Are there measures? Can they look back and say that over the past six months or over the past year we can see these steps were taken, these goals were accomplished? Men have a tendency to be objective and they want to see some results. Make sure this is part of the group's established plan. The results will be more productive.

85. Scripture Reading: Proverbs 27:17

DISCRETION

D iscretion is critical in your recovery. Identify the appropriate people whom you can trust with your story. Just as important is knowing the people to whom you should not reveal your addiction.

As much as pornography is currently talked about in the media and on talk shows, you have the right to privacy regarding your addiction and the details of your life. It is something that needs to be handled in an appropriate manner. It's much different than someone revealing a New Year's resolution to exercise more or to lose weight or to give up smoking. Those seem to be more socially acceptable lifestyle changes. But if you say to someone in the office or at a church group that you are going to give up pornography, be prepared for a vastly different response from folks. Make sure that the group with whom you share about your addiction is receptive to what you are revealing. Identify that this is an appropriate group of people and venue in which to air the details of your addiction.

In addition, remember to deal sensitively and appropriately with other people who have addictions. It's not your job to "save" the world because you are on the path to recovery. There are differences in addictions, how people handle them, and how society views them. Be careful that this type of interaction doesn't set you back and hurt you, sending you back into isolation. You need to do things that build on the sense of freedom that you are now enjoying since you have begun the process of recovery.

Points to Consider

1. What places would be appropriate and not appropriate for me to share about my addiction?
2. What is my motive for wanting to share with someone? Am I doing it to look good, or am I doing it to get the help I need?
3. What damage or what good would come from sharing?

86. Scripture Reading: Proverbs 3:21-22

THERAPY PROCESS

Therapy is a very effective tool if you find a therapist who understands what you are dealing with in regard to your addiction to pornography. Selecting a therapist will require some time, which may include consulting with your insurance and interviewing two or three prospective therapists. When interviewing therapists, it is appropriate to inquire on their specialties and experience. There are therapists who specialize in sexual addictions, and they can provide you with the help you need.

The therapy process needs to be genuine. You need to be open and your therapist needs to know everything about your addiction. Your therapist should not be judgmental, and meeting with him needs to feel safe. You need someone who will understand the nature of your addiction and will provide you with the skills and tools you need to overcome it. The therapist needs to be someone who does more than just listen, and you need a trained professional who doesn't constantly engage in Bible thumping and preaching, which turns off many men to the therapy process.

You must develop a genuine relationship with a therapist who can help keep you accountable. He needs to listen to your pain and understand what feeds and triggers the addiction. He needs to know why you do what you do and then provide you with ways to work toward recovery. You need to feel empowered so you can say, "I can make progress, even if in the beginning it is just baby steps." You should believe that there is hope and get beyond that you are constantly operating in a vacuum.

Therapy works for many people. It may take some men a long time or a dramatic incident before they come to the breaking point where they turn to a therapist. I encourage you to not wait until that point. Seek and receive therapy as soon as possible so that the pain is less and the journey to recovery is shorter.

Please know that any experienced therapist is not going to be shocked by what you reveal to him. In my practice, I have seen hundreds of men who have been involved in sexual sin on every possible level. No matter how grotesque your habits or how deep you are into your addiction, you need to find someone you can trust and with whom you can be completely open and honest. I believe it is best that men, especially those with sexual addictions, see male therapists. The Bible talks about men seeking out the elders in their church and community. Talking with a female therapist could lead to transference, which occurs when a patient receives a sexual charge when discussing his problem, especially if he speaks graphically to her. You need to find a godly man who will understand you and deal with your addiction man to man.

Many men will think that if they have had three sessions with a therapist, if they have removed the pornography from their home and computer, and if they have confessed the addiction to their wives, they are done. "Let's move on; let's do something different. I don't need to continue coming to therapy." Please remember that an addiction is an addiction—and you need to know the nature of the addiction. Therefore, therapy usually lasts anywhere from six months to a year, sometimes longer, on a weekly basis.

Do not be surprised if your therapist tries to deal with the root of the issue, the basis of the problem, and the triggers for your addiction. To go to therapy only two or three times may be helpful, but it will not address the core issues, and you run the risk of the addiction returning—sometimes even stronger than before.

Points to Consider

1. What do you want in a therapy process?
2. What are you afraid of?
3. Who would you go to for therapy, and how would you contact him so you can take the necessary steps to receive the professional help you deserve?

87. Scripture Reading: Isaiah 57:18

OVERCOMING THE ADDICTION · 201

ACCOUNTABILITY TO GOD

Everyone needs to realize that there will be a day when each of us will stand before our Lord and we will be accountable for the choices we have made. The addiction to pornography sometimes causes a man's conscience to become numb. You rationalize, justify, and excuse your use of pornography. You have worked hard to convince yourself that it's no big deal and has had no long-term affect on your life.

The Bible talks about the eyes being blind or calloused; so is the conscience. In 1 Timothy 4:2, the Lord talks about being calloused and the conscience being seared. One of things that you need to examine in your addiction is what you are doing and the impact that it is having on your life. You need to consider the implications of your actions. You are accountable in how you treat your wife. You are accountable in how you raise your children. You are accountable in how you walk your Christian walk and how you demonstrate the fruits of the Spirit.

Whether any one of us wants to accept it or not, there is a Day of Judgment for each person born into this world. There will be a time when your life and heart will be examined for those things that you have chosen to devote your life to. We need to be serious about this eventuality and not ignore it or think that we will live in the forgiveness of Christ every day and play him as a fool. Our Lord is not a fool—we are the ones who sometimes make foolish choices and then must live with the consequences of our behavior.

Consider your legacy and how you want to be remembered by your family, neighbors, church friends, and business colleagues. I think of a friend who lost her husband suddenly. He was a man in his early forties with a family and successful career. When his wife went through his wallet, briefcase, office desk, and computer files to finalize his estate and work matters, there was the potential to unearth many ungodly things. But this was a man of integrity who loved his wife and family—and respected himself. She found nothing that would blemish his good name or the proud legacy he left behind. I pray that this will be your legacy as well.

Points to Consider
1. Is your conscience numb, seared, hardened?
2. Do you believe you will be accountable, and for what?
3. If it happened today, would you be ready to face the Lord?

88. Scripture Reading: 1 Timothy 4:2; Romans 14:12

ACCOUNTABILITY TO HER

M en, we have made a commitment, a vow, and a covenant with our wives through our wedding vows and our profession of love. Women feel very violated when they discover that their husbands have indulged in pornography. You are accountable not just after you are caught, but before as well.

Is your heart pure? Is your wedding bed undefiled? I truly believe that women have a sixth sense. In counseling I have heard many wives say, "I've known all along, but I just didn't want to face it. I suspected something. Yes, he's changed and I had noticed the changes in him."

Men need to be accountable not just in a legalistic sense. Your heart not only needs to be in love with your wife—it needs to be held in check. Is she your first priority? Is she the first love of your heart? Do you cherish her as a human being, not just as a sexual partner? Do you value her and hold her in the highest esteem? Are you her protector, her guard, her covering? Are you the man of God she needs? Are you the type of husband with whom your wife wants to express her love with all her heart and her emotions as well as her body?

Marriage is a commitment, and a long-term marriage takes effort. It takes time, it takes creativity, and sometimes it needs some help. You have to willfully choose to love her every day for the rest of your life. You have to work at it every day in a gentle, caring, romantic way that meets her needs as well as yours.

Points to Consider

1. Does your wife really know you? Are there any secrets?
2. Do you cherish and value her completely?
3. In what ways are you accountable to each other?

89. Scripture Reading: Hebrews 13:4

ACCOUNTABILITY TO SELF

Who are you kidding? Your use of pornography is always a secret, one that you don't share with anyone. You have worked hard to keep your activities hidden. You shove your materials in a box in the garage or create special passwords or firewalls on the computer to prevent intruders from discovering your secret.

Yet you yourself know. In your heart you are aware of the lies you are telling, the sins you are committing, the secrets you are hiding. These erode your confidence, self-esteem, your sexual confidence, your ability to be creative and loving in the ways you should. The addiction is stifling, and at times it undermines your ability to work or to enjoy hobbies. It can even squeeze out the things you once found great joy doing because of the time you are spending with the pornography. It may be robbing you of sleep or other activities necessary for self-care.

Be accountable to yourself. Stand up on your own two feet and proclaim: "This is not who I want to be. I need to get this addiction out of my life. It's destructive. It's time consuming. It's expensive. There is no godly good that comes from my use of pornography. Therefore, I am going to stand up and get some help to stop my addiction. I'm going to stop doing what I know is wrong."

Points to Consider

1. Have you ever looked in the mirror and said, "This needs to stop!"?
2. What are you hiding and why?

3. Do you realize how destructive this is to yourself as well
    as to the others around you?

90. Scripture Reading: Hebrews 13:18

CHAPTER 5

STAYING VICTORIOUS

"How could I have been so deceived?" Tim asked. As we sat together sharing a cup of coffee, this thirty-year-old man with the cherubic face and I looked back over the time we had known each other. We met eight years ago when he called my office and said he was going to kill himself. He'd heard of my practice that deals with sexual addictions and wanted to find out if there was any hope for him. If not, he was going to take a bottle of sleeping pills and escape.

The next weeks and months were filled with intense therapy that included Tim and his wife, Juliet. For a while I thought their marriage was over, but God's grace and many miracles pulled it back from destruction. Tim stayed in one-on-one therapy and accountability groups for five years before he felt "healed" from his addiction to pornography. He's filled his life with positive people and healthy habits. Tim and Juliet have a thriving marriage, and they just adopted a beautiful infant boy. Tim now understands how he was deceived and how he became addicted to pornography while an undergraduate. Even more important, he knows how to live a life that is victorious. In fact, Tim has gone back to school and is training to become a youth counselor to help teens and young men avoid being caught in the traps that snared him.

IT NEVER GOES AWAY

I truly believe that all addictions—alcohol, gambling, drugs, pornography—never go away.

Therefore, part of staying victorious is to never turn your back and try to convince yourself that you will never again fall down. Once you think that you are "over" it and that you could dabble in any of your former activities, you will be consumed again and brought down. You have exposed your Achilles heel—your weakness—and set yourself up for attack by your own carelessness and foolishness. Never tell yourself: "I am over it, and the addiction is gone forever."

An addiction stays with you, dormant, until it seizes the opportunity to infiltrate your life again. You must guard your heart, you need to protect your marriage, you need to keep your eyes where they belong, and you have to continue to discipline yourself. It is never really over and the attraction to the addiction never goes away.

If the temptations begin to bubble to the surface, go back and reread the "Overcoming the Addiction" section of this book. I foresee that you may have to do this at points during the coming years. It's OK. You realize that you need a refresher. That's much better than a relapse. Call upon the Lord for strength. Communicate to your wife or a trusted friend. Don't isolate yourself. Be open so that you can have the support you need.

Points to Consider

1. Do you think your addiction has gone away?
2. Am I kidding myself?
3. How do I keep my heart, my marriage, and my eyes guarded?

91. Scripture Reading: 1 Corinthians 10:13

THE STRUGGLE CONTINUES

B y their very nature, addictions are controlling. They dictate your life. It's important to know that while the struggle continues, it will get better over time. The longer you go without the thing to which you are addicted, the better off you will be.

But you must be ever mindful of what triggers you. If it is stress, go exercise. A good workout will clear and strengthen both the body and the mind. Go talk with someone or do something that relaxes you. If it is anger, deal with the anger straight on; address the real cause rather than transferring or shoving down the feelings and covering the anger with your addictive behavior.

Knowing that the struggle with your addiction will be a part of your life doesn't demonstrate weakness. It shows your awareness and that you are giving the knowledge priority while giving the addiction itself as little space in your life as possible. By acknowledging that the snare could catch you easily, you are able to look at and tell yourself that you are OK. You can say, "I know that I'm going to make it through this weekend. I'm going to make it past this lonely spell. I am going to make healthy choices rather than delving into my past unhealthy pastimes of using pornography."

Set some short-term, realistic goals. You might opt for the following: For this one week, I can go completely without any type of pornography. Then you can look back and say, "There, I did it." Now set a goal of going two weeks, three weeks, then a month. Build on your success rather

than looking at your failures. Setting goals to deal with the
constant struggle is staying victorious.

Points to Consider

1. How do I know when I am vulnerable to falling back into
   my addiction?
2. What will I do when I feel drawn to pornography?
3. What are some short-term goals I can set for myself?

92. *Scripture Reading: Romans 13:13-14*

WHAT DOES HEALTHY LOOK LIKE?

Playing off a phrase in the movie *Forrest Gump*, you could say: "Healthy is as healthy does." This is a good foundation for everyone, not just those who are recovering from an addiction. People need to make their whole lives healthy. Keep your finances in order. Keep your house in order. Keep your career in order. Keep your mind, your sexuality, and your habits in order.

I am not suggesting you go to a compulsive level, but I am encouraging you to get to the point where you can say, "My life is in order. I have control over most aspects of my life." When you are in control of these other areas, you will find that it is much easier to be in control of your addiction to pornography. You will know your stopping and starting points for each day. You can say, "I know my destiny. I know what God wants me to do, and I feel that I am fulfilling my duties and the purpose for my life."

Dare to think of the future in different ways: "Because the addiction is now gone and I am staying victorious, what are my new dreams? If I have a new set of wings and I am free, where would I like to fly? What could I do now that the addiction held me back from accomplishing?" Enjoy the healthy path you have taken for your life.

Points to Consider
1. What needs to be put into complete order in your life?
2. What do healthy people look like, living day-to-day as intended?
3. What do I need to change to be more healthy?

93. Scripture Reading: Proverbs 21:21

214 · CONQUERING PORNOGRAPHY:
OVERCOMING THE ADDICTION

STAY THE PLAN

E very person coming off of an addiction needs to have a plan. The plan should include answers to questions such as the following:

- What am I going to do when my wife goes out of town for the weekend?
- What am I going to when I am at work and have some downtime and no one is around to see what I am viewing on the Internet?
- What am I going to do *instead* of the pornography?

If you are on a business trip, have activities scheduled for the evenings with colleagues or business associates. Or you could plan to go to a movie, a specialty store, a museum, or some unique cultural event the city has to offer. It doesn't matter what you choose to do, but it must be a proactive plan to keep yourself from falling into the addictive behavior.

Pornography is oftentimes considered a reactive behavior. If you had time, motivation, opportunity, etc., then you would look at the pornographic materials. In fact, while you were involved in your addiction, you would look forward to or even set special times when you could engage in the pornography. Now you need to make a plan to avoid it and to fill your mind and spirit with positive things that will enhance your life. Have goals and activities established so that you will not be caught in situations that will compromise your resolve to stay victorious.

Part of a successful plan is having an accountability partner, someone who on a regular basis asks you, "How are you doing?" Another key component of a plan is to have one or two people (someone other than your wife) who encourage you, pray with or for you, and are on your side. These should be your champions and partners in your recovery process, people who will say, "I think what you are doing is great, and I'm going to help you stay the course."

Finally, for a plan to be truly successful, you need to identify some rewards for accomplishing your plan. What would you reward yourself with for staying away from pornography? How much money will you save by abandoning this habit? How much time will you have available now for your family or favorite activities that you put aside when you were deep in your addiction? When you see the positive outcomes, you will know that you have created a plan with a solid foundation.

Points to Consider
1. What is my plan?
2. In what circumstances would I absolutely need a plan? What situations, excuses, or environments most often lured me into using pornography?
3. Is my plan feasible for healthy living, or does it have holes in it that might cause me to stumble?

94. Scripture Reading: Proverbs 14:22-23

THE GOOD STUFF

The good stuff is having so much emotional and spiritual freedom from this addiction that you develop a relationship with your wife that is beyond the high that you achieved when you viewed pornography. You will have a relationship with someone who is real, who breathes and talks, a person you can touch and with whom you can be in touch emotionally, physically, and spiritually.

That's the good stuff. It's the stuff that replaces the garbage. And then you realize: "What was I thinking? Why did I live that lie when now I am so much more content and happy?"

So if you think you are going to lose that high you had from pornography, you don't really know how high you can go until you have a healthy relationship. A healthy marriage that is truly of God is pure, is fun, and is freeing.

Points to Consider

1. How am I going to build that relationship with my wife?
2. What is the good stuff going to look like in my life? How would I describe it? What does it mean to me?
3. How am going to enjoy the change in my life? How will I thank God and my wife every day I am no longer in that bondage?

95. Scripture Reading: Philippians 4:8-9

HELPING OTHERS

When you give of yourself, it always comes back to you exponentially. You grow, they grow, and everyone is better for the connection. By giving to them, you feel better about yourself, and you feel better about the purpose of your life. Pornography is a very selfish and self-centered activity. The focus is on you and is certainly not helping anyone.

When you give to your neighbors, your family, the church, any organization, or to someone else in need, you become healthier and stronger. It takes your eyes off yourself and who you are. You will find that over time you will look back on your addiction and say to yourself: "What was I thinking? Why would I ever want to go back to doing those things and being that person when I can do things that are much more meaningful and actually help other people?"

Points to Consider

1. Which person or organization needs help right here, right now?
2. Where could I volunteer or give of myself that would allow me to take my eyes off myself and not be selfish?
3. Is there anyone else who shares my addiction to whom I could act as a mentor, coach, or sponsor and help pull him out of his addiction to pornography?

96. Scripture Reading: 2 Corinthians 9:13-15

RESPECTING HER

S taying victorious includes always regarding your precious wife as the loving, sweet woman she is to you. As a couple, you have been through a great battle together. Now you need to build her up and offer her your utmost respect.

Though we all have faults and have areas in which we need to grow, it is critical that you cherish her and work to rebuild the relationship. You need to focus on her in every aspect of your life, making her second only to God in giving her your love and time.

Communicate with her. Ask her what she needs physically, emotionally, and spiritually. Ask her what it will take for her to trust you. Ask her what needs to be done to heal your marriage. Listen with your heart and respond to her requests. Approach this new chapter in your life with enthusiasm and vigor.

Respecting her is staying victorious. You need to cultivate a deep and personal friendship with her. She should be your only lover—and she should be made to feel confident that you want to be with her only. You need to give her the dignity she deserves.

Points to Consider

1. How could I respect my wife more?
2. What can I do continually to uplift her and hold her in high esteem?
3. How can I assure her that being with her is much more satisfying than engaging in pornography?

97. Scripture Reading: Ephesians 5:25-28

BUILDING RELATIONSHIPS OUTSIDE

The way to stay healthy, which is the emphasis of this final section of the book, is making healthy choices. The first step, which I have covered earlier, is to make amends with your wife and strengthen that important relationship. In addition, you need to create relationships with people outside of your marriage that are healthy, fun, interactive, intellectual, and social. Friends and activities that give you something better to live for and to occupy your time and mind.

You are choosing to replace the pornography with a healthy lifestyle. That includes healthy people—folks who do not want to engage in lewd jokes or discussion of anything to do with pornography. You want to be with people who will uplift you and your wife, people who will stretch you emotionally, psychologically, and intellectually. You want things to be new and fresh.

Staying victorious is staying healthy. That means having relationships that are away from the pornography. The best way to make new friends is to find others who have a common interest. If you like bowling, join a bowling league. If you like bicycling, locate a bike club in your area. If you like golf, ask men at work or at church if they would like to play a round this Saturday. For men who tend to be shy, start out small. Seek out one person with whom you could develop a friendship through a common activity. But you have to step out. If you are isolated and lonely, the pornography has the potential to once again be your friend.

Couples need to meet other couples through common interests. Some people meet through church. While that is an effective way to make connections, that is not the only way. Look for avenues, such as places or organizations where you can serve or volunteer. The opportunities are endless if you will look around with fresh eyes to see a world beyond your addiction.

Points to Consider

1. What kind of friends would I like to make that are new and fresh?
2. What relationships could I build to make them stronger than they already are?
3. How could I grow if I were to make new friends and engage in new activities that would stimulate me and make my life more fulfilling?

98. Scripture Reading: Philippians 1:27

WALK WITH GOD

Walking with our Lord is staying victorious. It's knowing that you could never have overcome your addiction in the flesh, on your own. It's through the Holy Spirit and your relationship with Christ that you will stay victorious. Success will come to you through reading the Bible, attending healthy activities through church, and having relationships that glorify God.

It's walking with the Lord and saying, "Father, every day I want to stay victorious. I want to be glorifying to you. I want to give you the credit for my success."

Points to Consider

1. How is my relationship with God going to grow even more?
2. Day by day, am I being fed healthy material?
3. Do I thank the Lord for freeing me and helping me overcome my addiction?

99. Scripture Reading: 2 Corinthians 7:1

REDO THE WORK

S taying victorious means that you have to continually redo the work. You have to ask yourself, "Where am I weak? What is my downfall? Where can I shore up my life so that this doesn't happen again? What can I avoid so that I don't fall back into my addiction?"

By redoing the work, you are telling yourself that you are never going to let your eyes be shut to the fact that you have an addiction. But you are going to bolster your self-esteem and discover ways you can better yourself and improve your life, your marriage, and your relationships. You must make a conscious decision that you will stay away from the "monster" that bit you and tried to destroy your life.

You need to take steps of resolve: "I will put safeguards on my computer so I won't go to the sites I used to visit. I'm going to choose different types of movies so I don't slip into viewing soft pornography under the guise of 'it's only an R-rating.' I'm going to walk the walk of an overcomer. I'm going to make better and healthier choices day in and day out. I will know that I am victorious."

Points to Consider
1. What work do I need to redo, what steps do I need to retake?
2. How can I keep myself totally aware so that I am not drawn back into the addiction?
3. How can I pass this along to someone else so they can become stronger too?

100. Scripture Reading: Jude 1:20-23

SPIRITUAL WARFARE: TEMPTATIONS

When each of us is trying to overcome a habit, to grow in the Lord, to become more dedicated, or to enter into doing service work for him, anything that is kingdom-driven, Satan is going to try to fight and cause you to fail. He will attempt to prevent you from moving forward and overcoming the addiction. To be frank, Satan and his cohorts will try to sabotage the good work you are doing—and he will delight in your defeat. So don't be surprised when you are in the middle of your therapy or you are working your program* and you are trying to be victorious over pornography, that the temptation to lapse becomes even stronger and more persistent. The devil does not want you to succeed, but the Lord certainly does. And so do your wife, family, and friends.

This phase of your recovery is much like finally buying that special new, red car. All of a sudden you see that all the cars on the road look just like yours. Before, you never noticed the popularity of this model. The same is true when you start to become victorious. Your eyes are open, your heart is open, and you are more sensitive to everything out there. The struggle appears to be harder, but in reality you are working your program the strongest.

Do not give up. You will get through this dark time and you will pass through the tunnel. At the end you will find an immense amount of freedom.

Points to Consider

1. Have you seen your temptations increase once you began working to overcome the addiction to pornography?
2. Don't be afraid of the temptations. Who do you have to support you?
3. Are you calling upon the Lord to give you the strength you need to get past the temptation?

*"Working your program" is defined as the plan devised by you and your therapist, accountability group, or by yourself through reading this book to identify and attack your addiction and then achieve victory over it through a specialized program. For example, in my practice we call it the Conquering Pornography Program.

101. Scripture Reading: 1 Timothy 6:11

CELEBRATE YOUR SUCCESS

G o ahead, pat yourself on the back and celebrate your success. Mark the anniversary of when you walked away from your addiction to pornography. Remember the day you cleaned out the house, garage, or computer. Now that it has been 90 days, six months, or one year, you should mark the event with something special.

In AA, they mark the first month, two months, or first year of sobriety. Set up a time frame and establish a date on which you can note the occasion of being "sober" from your addiction to pornography. You can celebrate by going out to dinner or doing something romantic with your wife. Perhaps you can buy yourself a treat. You want to do something that says, "I did this and I want to celebrate!"

Even after a week or two of success, call a buddy and plan to attend a sporting event or take your wife out to dinner. Maybe after a month or two, you can go on a fishing trip with your brother or some guys from church. It's important to celebrate your successes.

Buy yourself a gift—something personal or for the house, like a shiny new riding lawnmower. Do whatever you would consider to be a reward. Celebrate your success with your wife. A reward for both of you would be to go away for the weekend. Do something that says to yourself and to her: "I was once like that, but I'm not into that behavior any longer. We're going to celebrate, and I'm going to thank the Lord that he has given me the strength to overcome."

Amidst your celebration, be sure to include the Lord, the one who gave you the strength and holds you dear, and the one who uplifts you every day and protects you. Give him praise and make him part of your celebration.

Also include family and friends who have been supportive of your recovery. Bring them around and have a joyful time. Your actions will show the appreciation you feel for their support and will demonstrate the changes you have made in your behavior.

By celebrating your victories, the act of overcoming will be more worthwhile. You won't spend time missing your addiction, missing your old habits, missing your old friends. Now you have put something better in its place. You are really living and enjoying life in all its fullness.

Points to Consider

1. What would be rewarding to me?
2. What would she consider to be a reward for her?
3. How can we celebrate my success of being free of my addiction?
4. What would be a special celebration for you? What would you particularly enjoy?
5. How often do you want to highlight your victories by having celebrations?
6. How will you include the Lord and your friends in your recovery celebration?

102. Scripture Reading: Philippians 3:13-14

PRACTICAL STEPS

H ere are some practical steps to help you avoid slipping back into your former habits.

- When you are on the computer and feel the temptation to look at pornography, get up and leave. Walk away from the temptation. The same applies to television programs, DVDs, or print material.
- Say a prayer and rebuke the pornography and temptation in the name of Jesus. Say it aloud.
- Call a friend or talk with your wife openly. Create a situation so that you are not alone.

Points to Consider

1. Will you be willing to walk away from the computer if you feel tempted?
2. Do you understand what it means to rebuke the temptation? Do you need to speak with a pastor to learn more about this type of prayer?
3. With whom are you going to speak? You should have a list of at least five people so that someone will always be available to talk with you immediately.

103. Scripture Reading: Philippians 2:12-13; Colossians 2:6-8

STEPS TO RECOVERY

You can get past the addiction and achieve victory!

- Admit it—bring the problem out in the open.
- Own it—stop blaming everyone else (no excuses).
- Quit cold turkey—no stepping down gradually.
- Clean house—search and destroy all traces of pornography.
- Develop real relationships to replace pornographic ones.
- Set up some accountability (other than with your wife).
- Find help and begin to achieve healthy relationships.
- Stay active and involved with healthy activities—fill your time with positive alternatives.
- Focus on something besides you.
- Have a plan for when you're tempted.
- Never turn your back on this addiction and think you're cured.
- Realize it will be a long, rough road, but it's worth it!
- Develop an honest and strong relationship with God, and ask the Holy Spirit to intercede for you.
- *Never* be afraid to ask for help.

Print this page and put it in your briefcase, the glove compartment of your car, next to your computer, or in your journal or Bible.

APPENDIX

APPENDIX A: SCRIPTURE READINGS

Introduction

1. Philippians 3:20-21

But our citizenship is in heaven. And we eagerly await a Savior from there, the Lord Jesus Christ, who, by the power that enables him to bring everything under his control, will transform our lowly bodies so that they will be like his glorious body.

Chapter 1: How You Got Hooked

2. Judges 16:1

One day Samson went to Gaza, where he saw a prostitute. He went in to spend the night with her.

3. *Proverbs 27:20*

Death and destruction are never satisfied, and neither are the eyes of man.

4. *Song of Songs 4:1-5*

How beautiful you are, my darling! Oh, how beautiful! Your eyes behind your veil are doves. Your hair is like a flock of goats descending from Mount Gilead. Your teeth are like a flock of sheep just shorn, coming up from the washing. Each has its twin; not one of them is alone. Your lips are like a scarlet ribbon; your mouth is lovely. Your temples behind your veil are like the halves of a pomegranate. Your neck is like the tower of David, built with elegance; on it hang a thousand shields, all of them shields of warriors. Your two breasts are like two fawns, like twin fawns of a gazelle that browse among the lilies.

5. *1 John 2:16*

For everything in the world—the cravings of sinful man, the lust of his eyes and the boasting of what he has and does—comes not from the Father but from the world.

6.a. *Mark 7:21-22*

For from within, out of men's hearts, come evil thoughts, sexual immorality, theft, murder, adultery, greed, malice, deceit, lewdness, envy, slander, arrogance and folly.

6.b. *Colossians 3:5*

Put to death, therefore, whatever belongs to your earthly nature: sexual immorality, impurity, lust, evil desires and greed, which is idolatry.

7. 1 Corinthians 6:15-20

Do you not know that your bodies are members of Christ himself? Shall I then take the members of Christ and unite them with a prostitute? Never! Do you not know that he who unites himself with a prostitute is one with her in body? For it is said, "The two will become one flesh." But he who unites himself with the Lord is one with him in spirit. Flee from sexual immorality. All other sins a man commits are outside his body, but he who sins sexually sins against his own body. Do you not know that your body is a temple of the Holy Spirit, who is in you, whom you have received from God? You are not your own; you were bought at a price. Therefore honor God with your body.

8. Isaiah 44:9

All who make idols are nothing, and the things they treasure are worthless. Those who would speak up for them are blind; they are ignorant, to their own shame.

9. Colossians 3:5

Put to death, therefore, whatever belongs to your earthly nature: sexual immorality, impurity, lust, evil desires and greed, which is idolatry.

10. Ephesians 4:15-19

Instead, speaking the truth in love, we will in all things grow up into him who is the Head, that is, Christ. From him the whole body, joined and held together by every supporting ligament, grows and builds itself up in love, as each part does its work. So I tell you this, and insist on it in the Lord, that you must no longer live as the Gentiles do, in the futility of their thinking. They are darkened in their understanding and separated from the life of God because of the ignorance that is in them due to the hardening of their hearts. Having lost all sensitivity, they have given themselves over to sensuality so as to indulge in every kind of impurity, with a continual lust for more.

11. Isaiah 55:7

Let the wicked forsake his way and the evil man his thoughts. Let him turn to the Lord, and he will have mercy on him, and to our God, for he will freely pardon.

12. 2 Corinthians 10:5

We demolish arguments and every pretension that sets itself up against the knowledge of God, and we take captive every thought to make it obedient to Christ.

13. Hebrews 4:12-13

For the word of God is living and active. Sharper than any double-edged sword, it penetrates even to dividing soul and spirit, joints and marrow; it judges the thoughts and attitudes of the heart. Nothing in all creation is hidden from God's sight. Everything is uncovered and laid bare before the eyes of him to whom we must give account.

14.a. Numbers 14:18

The Lord is slow to anger, abounding in love and forgiving sin and rebellion. Yet he does not leave the guilty unpunished; he punishes the children for the sin of the fathers to the third and fourth generation.

14.b. Matthew 18:6

But if anyone causes one of these little ones who believe in me to sin, it would be better for him to have a large millstone hung around his neck and to be drowned in the depths of the sea.

15. Isaiah 54:4a

"Do not be afraid; you will not suffer shame. Do not fear disgrace; you will not be humiliated."

16. Psalms 59:1-4

Deliver me from my enemies, O God; protect me from those who rise up against me. Deliver me from evildoers and save me from bloodthirsty men. See how they lie in wait for me! Fierce men conspire against me for no offense or sin of mine, O Lord. I have done no wrong, yet they are ready to attack me. Arise to help me; look on my plight!

17. 1 Corinthians 7:8-9

Now to the unmarried and the widows I say: It is good for them to stay unmarried, as I am. But if they cannot control themselves, they should marry, for it is better to marry than to burn with passion.

18. Psalms 35:1-4

Contend, O Lord, with those who contend with me; fight against those who fight against me. Take up shield and buckler; arise and come to my aid. Brandish spear and javelin against those who pursue me. Say to my soul, "I am your salvation." May those who seek my life be disgraced and put to shame; may those who plot my ruin be turned back in dismay.

Chapter 2: The Effect on Self, Women, and Others

19. Isaiah 44:9

All who make idols are nothing, and the things they treasure are worthless. Those who would speak up for them are blind; they are ignorant, to their own shame.

20. Romans 1:21-27

For although they knew God, they neither glorified him as God nor gave thanks to him, but their thinking became futile and their foolish hearts were darkened. Although they claimed to be wise, they became fools and exchanged the glory of the immortal God for images made to look like mortal man and birds and animals and reptiles. Therefore God gave them over in the sinful desires of their hearts to sexual impurity for the degrading of their bodies with one another. They exchanged the truth of God for a lie, and worshiped and served created things rather than the Creator—who is forever praised. Amen. Because of this, God gave them over to shameful lusts. Even their women exchanged natural relations for unnatural ones. In the same way the men also abandoned natural relations with women and were inflamed with lust for one another. Men committed indecent acts with other men, and received in themselves the due penalty for their perversion.

21. 1 Corinthians 6:15-20

Do you not know that your bodies are members of Christ himself? Shall I then take the members of Christ and unite them with a prostitute? Never! Do you not know that he who unites himself with a prostitute is one with her in body? For it is said, "The two will become one flesh." But he who unites himself with the Lord is one with him in spirit. Flee from sexual immorality. All other sins a man commits are outside his body, but he who sins sexually sins against his own body. Do you not know that your body is a temple of the Holy Spirit, who is in you, whom you have received from God? You are not your own; you were bought at a price. Therefore honor God with your body.

22. Ephesians 4:15-19

Instead, speaking the truth in love, we will in all things grow up into him who is the Head, that is, Christ. From him the whole body, joined and held together by every supporting ligament, grows and builds itself up in love, as each part does its work. So I tell you this, and insist on it in the Lord, that you must no longer live as the Gentiles do, in the futility of their thinking. They are darkened in their understanding and separated from the life of God because of the ignorance that is in them due to the hardening of their hearts. Having lost all sensitivity, they have given themselves over to sensuality so as to indulge in every kind of impurity, with a continual lust for more.

23. Deuteronomy 28:65-67

Among those nations you will find no repose, no resting place for the sole of your foot. There the Lord will give you an anxious mind, eyes weary with longing, and a despairing heart. You will live in constant suspense, filled with dread both night and day, never sure of your life. In the morning you will say, "If only it were evening!" and in the evening,

"If only it were morning!"—because of the terror that will fill your hearts and the sights that your eyes will see.

24. *Colossians 3:5-10*

Put to death, therefore, whatever belongs to your earthly nature: sexual immorality, impurity, lust, evil desires and greed, which is idolatry. Because of these, the wrath of God is coming. You used to walk in these ways, in the life you once lived. But now you must rid yourselves of all such things as these: anger, rage, malice, slander, and filthy language from your lips. Do not lie to each other, since you have taken off your old self with its practices and have put on the new self, which is being renewed in knowledge in the image of its Creator.

25.a. *Proverbs 11:21-22*

Be sure of this: The wicked will not go unpunished, but those who are righteous will go free. Like a gold ring in a pig's snout is a beautiful woman who shows no discretion.

25.b. *Psalm 112:1-6*

Praise the Lord. Blessed is the man who fears the Lord, who finds great delight in his commands. His children will be mighty in the land; the generation of the upright will be blessed. Wealth and riches are in his house, and his righteousness endures forever. Even in darkness light dawns for the upright, for the gracious and compassionate and righteous man. Good will come to him who is generous and lends freely, who conducts his affairs with justice. Surely he will never be shaken; a righteous man will be remembered forever.

26. Genesis 1:26-27

Then God said, "Let us make man in our image, in our likeness, and let them rule over the fish of the sea and the birds of the air, over the livestock, over all the earth, and over all the creatures that move along the ground." So God created man in his own image, in the image of God he created him; male and female he created them.

27. Galatians 5:19-21

The acts of the sinful nature are obvious: sexual immorality, impurity and debauchery; idolatry and witchcraft; hatred, discord, jealousy, fits of rage, selfish ambition, dissensions, factions and envy; drunkenness, orgies, and the like. I warn you, as I did before, that those who live like this will not inherit the kingdom of God.

28. Isaiah 65:6-7

See, it stands written before me: "I will not keep silent but will pay back in full; I will pay it back into their laps— both your sins and the sins of your fathers," says the Lord. "Because they burned sacrifices on the mountains and defied me on the hills, I will measure into their laps the full payment for their former deeds."

29.a. Matthew 18:6

But if anyone causes one of these little ones who believe in me to sin, it would be better for him to have a large millstone hung around his neck and to be drowned in the depths of the sea.

29.b. Proverbs 22:6

Train a child in the way he should go, and when he is old he will not turn from it.

30. 1 Corinthians 7:3-5

The husband should fulfill his marital duty to his wife, and likewise the wife to her husband. The wife's body does not belong to her alone but also to her husband. In the same way, the husband's body does not belong to him alone but also to his wife. Do not deprive each other except by mutual consent and for a time, so that you may devote yourselves to prayer. Then come together again so that Satan will not tempt you because of your lack of self-control.

31.a. Hebrews 13:4

Marriage should be honored by all, and kept pure, for God will judge the adulterer and all the sexually immoral.

31.b. Colossians 3:19

Husbands, love your wives and do not be harsh with them.

31.c. 1 Peter 3:7

Husbands, in the same way be considerate as you live with your wives, and treat them with respect as the weaker partner and as heirs with you of the gracious gift of life, so that nothing will hinder your prayers.

32.a. Genesis 1:26-27

Then God said, "Let us make man in our image, in our likeness, and let them rule over the fish of the sea and the birds of the air, over the livestock, over all the earth, and over all the creatures that move along the ground." So God created man in his own image, in the image of God he created him; male and female he created them.

32.b. 1 Corinthians 4:2

Now it is required that those who have been given a trust must prove faithful.

33.a. Proverbs 3:8

This will bring health to your body and nourishment to your bones.

34. Proverbs 5:20-23

Why be captivated, my son, by an adulteress? Why embrace the bosom of another man's wife? For a man's ways are in full view of the Lord, and he examines all his paths. The evil deeds of a wicked man ensnare him; the cords of his sin hold him fast. He will die for lack of discipline, led astray by his own great folly.

Chapter 3: The Secret, The Lie

35.a. Isaiah 45:16

All the makers of idols will be put to shame and disgraced; they will go off into disgrace together.

35.b. Daniel 9:8

O Lord, we and our kings, our princes and our fathers are covered with shame because we have sinned against you.

36.a. Matthew 15:19

For out of the heart come evil thoughts, murder, adultery, sexual immorality, theft, false testimony, slander.

36.b. Matthew 5:28

But I tell you that anyone who looks at a woman lustfully has already committed adultery with her in his heart.

37. Proverbs 6:23-29

For these commands are a lamp, this teaching is a light, and the corrections of discipline are the way to life, keeping you from the immoral woman, from the smooth tongue of the wayward wife. Do not lust in your heart after her beauty or let her captivate you with her eyes, for the prostitute reduces you to a loaf of bread, and the adulteress preys upon your very life. Can a man scoop fire into his lap without his clothes being burned? Can a man walk on hot coals without his feet being scorched? So is he who sleeps with another man's wife; no one who touches her will go unpunished.

38. Colossians 3:9

Do not lie to each other, since you have taken off your old self with its practices.

38.b. Ecclesiastes 10:12

Words from a wise man's mouth are gracious, but a fool is consumed by his own lips.

39. Deuteronomy 13:6-8

If your very own brother, or your son or daughter, or the wife you love, or your closest friend secretly entices you, saying, "Let us go and worship other gods" (gods that neither you nor your fathers have known, gods of the peoples around you, whether near or far, from one end of the land to the other), do not yield to him or listen to him. Show him no pity. Do not spare him or shield him.

40. 2 Peter 2:18-19

For they mouth empty, boastful words and, by appealing to the lustful desires of sinful human nature, they entice people who are just escaping from those who live in error. They promise them freedom, while they themselves are slaves of depravity—for a man is a slave to whatever has mastered him.

41. Romans 5:19

For just as through the disobedience of the one man the many were made sinners, so also through the obedience of the one man the many will be made righteous.

42. Romans 7:19-25

For what I do is not the good I want to do; no, the evil I do not want to do—this I keep on doing. Now if I do what I do not want to do, it is no longer I who do it, but it is sin living in me that does it. So I find this law at work: When I want to do good, evil is right there with me. For in my inner being I delight in God's law; but I see another law at work in the members of my body, waging war against the law of my mind and making me a prisoner of the law of sin at work within my members. What a wretched man I am! Who will rescue me from this body of death? Thanks be to God—through Jesus Christ our Lord! So then, I myself in

my mind am a slave to God's law, but in the sinful nature
a slave to the law of sin.

43. Luke 16:15

He said to them, "You are the ones who justify yourselves
in the eyes of men, but God knows your hearts. What is
highly valued among men is detestable in God's sight."

44. James 5:16

Therefore confess your sins to each other and pray
for each other so that you may be healed. The prayer of a
righteous man is powerful and effective.

45. 1 Thessalonians 4:3-5

It is God's will that you should be sanctified: that you
should avoid sexual immorality; that each of you should
learn to control his own body in a way that is holy and
honorable, not in passionate lust like the heathen, who do
not know God.

46. Job 36:8-12

But if men are bound in chains, held fast by cords of
affliction, he tells them what they have done—that they have
sinned arrogantly. He makes them listen to correction and
commands them to repent of their evil. If they obey and
serve him, they will spend the rest of their days in prosperity
and their years in contentment. But if they do not listen,
they will perish by the sword and die without knowledge.

47.a. Ezekiel 20:30

Therefore say to the house of Israel: "This is what the
Sovereign Lord says: 'Will you defile yourselves the way
your fathers did and lust after their vile images?'"

47.b. Philippians 4:8

Finally, brothers, whatever is true, whatever is noble, whatever is right, whatever is pure, whatever is lovely, whatever is admirable—if anything is excellent or praiseworthy—think about such things.

48. 1 Corinthians 6:13

"Food for the stomach and the stomach for food"—but God will destroy them both. The body is not meant for sexual immorality, but for the Lord, and the Lord for the body.

49. Matthew 6:20-23

But store up for yourselves treasures in heaven, where moth and rust do not destroy, and where thieves do not break in and steal. For where your treasure is, there your heart will be also. The eye is the lamp of the body. If your eyes are good, your whole body will be full of light. But if your eyes are bad, your whole body will be full of darkness. If then the light within you is darkness, how great is that darkness!

50.a. Galatians 6:1

Brothers and sisters, if someone is caught in a sin, you who live by the Spirit should restore that person gently. But watch yourselves, or you also may be tempted.

50.b. Psalms 119:133

Direct my footsteps according to your word; let no sin rule over me.

51. 1 Timothy 4:7-8

Have nothing to do with godless myths and old wives' tales; rather, train yourself to be godly. For physical training is of some value, but godliness has value for all things, holding promise for both the present life and the life to come.

52. Philippians 4:6-7

Do not be anxious about anything, but in everything, by prayer and petition, with thanksgiving, present your requests to God. And the peace of God, which transcends all understanding, will guard your hearts and your minds in Christ Jesus.

53. Psalm 31:9-10

Be merciful to me, O Lord, for I am in distress; my eyes grow weak with sorrow, my soul and my body with grief. My life is consumed by anguish and my years by groaning; my strength fails because of my affliction, and my bones grow weak.

54. Jeremiah 51:53

Even if Babylon reaches the sky and fortifies her lofty stronghold, I will send destroyers against her, declares the Lord.

55. Romans 1:28-32

Furthermore, since they did not think it worthwhile to retain the knowledge of God, he gave them over to a depraved mind, to do what ought not to be done. They have become filled with every kind of wickedness, evil, greed and depravity. They are full of envy, murder, strife, deceit and malice. They are gossips, slanderers, God-haters, insolent, arrogant and boastful; they invent ways of doing evil; they disobey their parents; they are senseless, faithless, heartless, ruthless. Although they know God's righteous decree that those who do such things deserve death, they not only continue to do these very things but also approve of those who practice them.

Chapter 4: Overcoming the Addiction

56. Acts 3:19

Repent, then, and turn to God, so that your sins may be wiped out, that times of refreshing may come from the Lord.

57.a. James 1:5

If any of you lacks wisdom, he should ask God, who gives generously to all without finding fault, and it will be given to him.

57.b. James 4:17

Anyone, then, who knows the good he ought to do and doesn't do it, sins.

58. Ephesians 4:19

Having lost all sensitivity, they have given themselves over to sensuality so as to indulge in every kind of impurity, with a continual lust for more.

59.a. 2 Corinthians 7:9

Yet now I am happy, not because you were made sorry, but because your sorrow led you to repentance. For you became sorrowful as God intended and so were not harmed in any way by us.

59.b. Romans 3:23

For all have sinned and fall short of the glory of God.

60. Matthew 12:43-45

"When an evil spirit comes out of a man, it goes through arid places seeking rest and does not find it. Then it says, 'I will return to the house I left.' When it arrives, it finds the house occupied, swept clean and put in order. Then it goes and takes with it seven other spirits more wicked than itself, and they go in and live there. And the final condition of that man is worse than the first. That is how it will be with this wicked generation."

61.a. Matthew 7:12

So in everything, do to others what you would have them do to you, for this sums up the Law and the Prophets.

61.b. Luke 6:31

Do to others as you would have them do to you.

62. Matthew 12:36

But I tell you that men will have to give account on the day of judgment for every careless word they have spoken.

63. James 5:16

Therefore confess your sins to each other and pray for each other so that you may be healed. The prayer of a righteous man is powerful and effective.

64.a. 1 Corinthians 6:18

Flee from sexual immorality. All other sins a man commits are outside his body, but he who sins sexually sins against his own body.

64.b. Matthew 5:28-29

But I tell you that anyone who looks at a woman lustfully has already committed adultery with her in his heart. If your right eye causes you to sin, gouge it out and throw it away. It is better for you to lose one part of your body than for your whole body to be thrown into hell.

65. James 2:26

As the body without the spirit is dead, so faith without deeds is dead.

66. Philippians 4:13

I can do everything through him who gives me strength.

67.a. Hebrews 10:22

Let us draw near to God with a sincere heart in full assurance of faith, having our hearts sprinkled to cleanse us from a guilty conscience and having our bodies washed with pure water.

67.b. 2 Timothy 2:21

If a man cleanses himself from the latter, he will be an instrument for noble purposes, made holy, useful to the Master and prepared to do any good work.

68. *2 Corinthians 12:21*

I am afraid that when I come again my God will humble me before you, and I will be grieved over many who have sinned earlier and have not repented of the impurity, sexual sin and debauchery in which they have indulged.

69. *Mark 14:38*

"Watch and pray so that you will not fall into temptation. The spirit is willing, but the body is weak."

70. *1 Corinthians 5:7*

Get rid of the old yeast that you may be a new batch without yeast—as you really are. For Christ, our Passover lamb, has been sacrificed.

71. *Romans 1:28-32*

Furthermore, since they did not think it worthwhile to retain the knowledge of God, he gave them over to a depraved mind, to do what ought not to be done. They have become filled with every kind of wickedness, evil, greed and depravity. They are full of envy, murder, strife, deceit and malice. They are gossips, slanderers, God-haters, insolent, arrogant and boastful; they invent ways of doing evil; they disobey their parents; they are senseless, faithless, heartless, ruthless. Although they know God's righteous decree that those who do such things deserve death, they not only continue to do these very things but also approve of those who practice them.

72. *Ephesians 4:26-27*

"In your anger do not sin": Do not let the sun go down while you are still angry, and do not give the devil a foothold.

73. *1 Corinthians 6:18-20*

Flee from sexual immorality. All other sins a man commits are outside his body, but he who sins sexually sins against his own body. Do you not know that your body is a temple of the Holy Spirit, who is in you, whom you have received from God? You are not your own; you were bought at a price. Therefore honor God with your body.

74. *Psalms 40:12*

For troubles without number surround me; my sins have overtaken me, and I cannot see. They are more than the hairs of my head, and my heart fails within me.

75. *1 John 2:16*

For everything in the world—the cravings of sinful man, the lust of his eyes and the boasting of what he has and does—comes not from the Father but from the world.

76. *Matthew 14:23*

After he had dismissed them, he went up on a mountainside by himself to pray. When evening came, he was there alone.

77. *Ephesians 5:3-12*

But among you there must not be even the hint of sexual immorality, or of any kind of impurity, or of greed, because these are improper for God's holy people. Nor should there be obscenity, foolish talk or coarse joking, which are out of place, but rather thanksgiving. For of this you can be sure: No immoral, impure or greedy person—such a man is an idolater—has any inheritance in the kingdom of Christ and of God. Let no one deceive you with empty words, for because of such things God's wrath comes on those who are disobedient. Therefore do not be partners with them. For you were once darkness, but now you are light in the Lord. Live as children of light (for the fruit of the light consists in all goodness, righteousness and truth) and find out what pleases the Lord. Have nothing to do with the fruitless deeds of darkness, but rather expose them. For it is shameful even to mention what the disobedient do in secret.

78.a. 1 John 1:9

If we confess our sins, he is faithful and just and will forgive us our sins and purify us from all unrighteousness.

78.b. Philippians 4:8-9

Finally, brothers, whatever is true, whatever is noble, whatever is right, whatever is pure, whatever is lovely, whatever is admirable—if anything is excellent or praiseworthy—think about such things. Whatever you have learned or received or heard from me, or seen in me—put it into practice. And the God of peace will be with you.

79. Galatians 5:1

It is for freedom that Christ has set us free. Stand firm, then, and do not let yourselves be burdened again by a yoke of slavery.

80.a 2 Timothy 2:22

Flee the evil desires of youth, and pursue righteousness, faith, love and peace, along with those who call on the Lord out of a pure heart.

80.b. Genesis 19:17

As soon as they had brought them out, one of them said, "Flee for your lives! Don't look back, and don't stop anywhere in the plain! Flee to the mountains or you will be swept away!"

81. James 1:14-16

But each one is tempted when, by his own evil desire, he is dragged away and enticed. Then, after desire has conceived, it gives birth to sin; and sin, when it is full-grown, gives birth to death. Don't be deceived, my dear brothers.

82.a. 1 Corinthians 7:2-3

But since there is so much immorality, each man should have his own wife, and each woman her own husband. The husband should fulfill his marital duty to his wife, and likewise the wife to her husband.

82.b. 1 Peter 3:7

Husbands, in the same way be considerate as you live with your wives, and treat them with respect as the weaker partner and as heirs with you of the gracious gift of life, so that nothing will hinder your prayers.

83. Proverbs 5:18-19

May your fountain be blessed, and may you rejoice in the wife of your youth. A loving doe, a graceful deer—may her breasts satisfy you always, may you ever be captivated by her love.

84. Daniel 9:3

So I turned to the Lord God and pleaded with him in prayer and petition, in fasting, and in sackcloth and ashes.

85. Proverbs 27:17

As iron sharpens iron, so one man sharpens another.

86. Proverbs 3:21-22

My son, preserve sound judgment and discernment, do not let them out of your sight; they will be life for you, an ornament to grace your neck.

87. Isaiah 57:18

I have seen his ways, but I will heal him; I will guide him and restore comfort to him.

88.a. 1 Timothy 4:2

Such teachings come through hypocritical liars, whose consciences have been seared as with a hot iron.

88.b. Romans 14:12

So then, each of us will give an account of himself to God.

89. Hebrews 13:4

Marriage should be honored by all, and the marriage bed kept pure, for God will judge the adulterer and all the sexually immoral.

90. Hebrews 13:18

Pray for us. We are sure that we have a clear conscience and desire to live honorably in every way.

Chapter 5: Staying Victorious

91. 1 Corinthians 10:13

No temptation has seized you except what is common to man. And God is faithful; he will not let you be tempted beyond what you can bear. But when you are tempted, he will also provide a way out so that you can stand up under it.

92. Romans 13:13-14

Let us behave decently, as in the daytime, not in orgies and drunkenness, not in sexual immorality and debauchery, not in dissension and jealousy. Rather, clothe yourselves with the Lord Jesus Christ, and do not think about how to gratify the desires of the sinful nature.

93. Proverbs 21:21

He who pursues righteousness and love finds life, prosperity and honor.

94. Proverbs 14:22-23

Do not those who plot evil go astray? But those who plan what is good find love and faithfulness. All hard work brings a profit, but mere talk leads only to poverty.

95. Philippians 4:8-9

Finally, brothers, whatever is true, whatever is noble, whatever is right, whatever is pure, whatever is lovely, whatever is admirable—if anything is excellent or praiseworthy—think about such things. Whatever you have learned or received or heard from me, or seen in me—put it into practice. And the God of peace will be with you.

96. 2 Corinthians 9:13-15

Because of the service by which you have proved yourselves, men will praise God for the obedience that accompanies your confession of the gospel of Christ, and for your generosity in sharing with them and with everyone else. And in their prayers for you their hearts will go out to you, because of the surpassing grace God has given you. Thanks be to God for his indescribable gift!

97. Ephesians 5:25-28

Husbands, love your wives, just as Christ loved the church and gave himself up for her to make her holy, cleansing her by the washing with water through the word, and to present her to himself as a radiant church, without stain or wrinkle or any other blemish, but holy and blameless. In this same way, husbands ought to love their wives as their own bodies. He who loves his wife loves himself.

98. Philippians 1:27

Whatever happens, conduct yourselves in a manner worthy of the gospel of Christ. Then, whether I come and see you or only hear about you in my absence, I will know that you stand firm in one spirit, contending as one man for the faith of the gospel.

99. 2 Corinthians 7:1

Since we have these promises, dear friends, let us purify ourselves from everything that contaminates body and spirit, perfecting holiness out of reverence for God.

100. Jude 1:20-23

But you, dear friends, build yourselves up in your most holy faith and pray in the Holy Spirit. Keep yourselves in God's love as you wait for the mercy of our Lord Jesus Christ to bring you to eternal life. Be merciful to those who doubt; snatch others from the fire and save them; to others show mercy, mixed with fear—hating even the clothing stained by corrupted flesh.

101. 1 Timothy 6:11

But you, man of God, flee from all this, and pursue righteousness, godliness, faith, love, endurance and gentleness.

102. Philippians 3:13-14

Brothers, I do not consider myself yet to have taken hold of it. But one thing I do: Forgetting what is behind and straining toward what is ahead, I press on toward the goal to win the prize for which God has called me heavenward in Christ Jesus.

103.a. Philippians 2:12-13

Therefore, my dear friends, as you have always obeyed—not only in my presence, but now much more in my absence—continue to work out your salvation with fear and trembling, for it is God who works in you to will and to act according to his good purpose.

103.b. Colossians 2:6-8

So then, just as you received Christ Jesus as Lord, continue to live in him, rooted and built up in him, strengthened in the faith as you were taught, and overflowing with thankfulness. See to it that no one takes you captive through hollow and deceptive philosophy, which depends on human tradition and the basic principles of this world rather than on Christ.

APPENDIX B: YOUR SPIRITUAL INVENTORY

"For everything comes from God alone. Everything lives
by his power, and everything is for his glory."
—Romans 11:36

Taking a spiritual inventory of yourself provides a time
of reflection and serious evaluation of your relationship
with God. It is personal and deep. It may take months
or a lifetime to truly understand how your one-on-one
relationship is to develop and become Christ-centered.
Following is a checklist to help you identify your current
relationship with God, the Father; Jesus Christ, the Son;
and the Holy Spirit.

The purpose of this exercise is not to be legalistic or
judgmental. There are no "right" and "wrong" answers. Let
it be customized to your personality and needs. Focus on
the key areas where you need to change and grow. Be honest
about your life and how your choices and activities affect
your recovery. The goal is to live a full and healthy life.

Take time and answer these questions as accurately and
honestly as possible. Revisit the checklist periodically to see
how you have grown and if there are areas where you need
to do additional work.

- Do I know I am loved by God?
- Where is my faith? Do I believe God has my best interest
  in his mind?
- Do I take the Bible seriously?
- Do I apply what I need to do?
- What is my prayer life like?

- What are my priorities?
- What relationships do I cherish?
- What relationships do I need to end?
- What are my barriers?
- Do I forgive others and myself—and God?
- What am I doing outside myself for the kingdom?
- Is the world a better place because of my existence?
- Am I proud?
- What idols do I covet?
- Do I show mercy to others and myself?
- What are my secrets?
- What am I holding on to that I need to release?
- What is the cost—financial, emotional, professional, relational—of my addiction?
- Do I believe that God has the power to free me from my addiction?
- Has the pain of my addiction become a friend?
- Do I praise and thank God for my progress?
- What are my goals?

APPENDIX C: RESOURCES

Treatment and Information

Tern Christian Counseling
33309 1st Way S., Suite 203
Federal Way, WA 98003-6260
Toll free: 1-866-952-2556
Web site: www.ternchristiancounseling.org

Focus on the Family
8655 Explorer Drive
Colorado Springs, CO 80920
Toll free: 1-800-232-6459
Web site: www.family.org

Internet Filtering Services
Integrity Online
Web site: www.integrity.com

Every Home Protected
Web site: www.everyhomeprotected.com

Monitoring Software
Web Watcher
Web site: www.awarenesstech.com/parents/index/html

Spector Pro 6.0

Web site: <u>www.spectorsoft.com/products/SpectorPro</u> <u>Windows/entry.asp?affil=479</u>

eBlaster 5.0

Web site: <u>www.spectorsoft.com</u>

Printed in the United States
81146LV00004B/1-111

9 781414 106175